www.itchybath.co.uk

Globe Quay Globe Road Leeds LS11 5QG
t: 0113 246 0440 f: 0113 246 0550 e: all@itchymedia.co.uk

City Editor	Tamla Walker
City Manager	Kelly Halborg
Editors	Simon Gray, Mike Waugh Andrew Wood, Ruby Quince
Design	Matt Wood , Chris McNamara
Photography	James Smith, Mikey Gooch
Acknowledgements	Pete, Kris, Jack, Sam, Charlie, Michael. Cat, Dog and Eric Nuff

The views expressed in this publication are those of the authors and contributors and are not necessarily those held by the editors or publishers. Readers are advised to form their own opinions and we welcome any contributions. All details, listings, addresses, phone numbers are correct to our knowledge at the time of going to print. itchy Ltd cannot be held responsible for any breach of copyright arising from the supply of artwork from advertisers.'

contents

top fives

Oh my God we're good to you...

Not only do we write funky little books but we also offer you, the discerning entertainment junkie, some pretty fine stuff on-line.

Point your browser to **www.itchycity.co.uk** and we'll not only keep you entertained with stories and reviews about what's going on in your city, we can also send you regular emails and SMS messages about the stuff you're into. So, we'll keep you informed about where the best happy hours are, when Oakenfold's next in town or where you can find a kebab at 2am. There's also a chance for you to contribute your views and reviews and get free stuff in return (we are too good to you). Have a shoofty. Go on.

itchy box set

Oh, imagine. **All 16 titles**, an encyclopaedia of entertainment across the country, all wrapped up in a glorious multi-coloured special box. Every title below in one mother of a box. Limited edition, naturally, and so exclusive, we don't even know what it looks like ourselves.

If you were to buy these individually, it'd cost you a bargainous £44. But hello, what's this? We're doing the full caboodle **for a mere £35**, including free postage and packing. **Call 0113 246 0440** and order by credit/debit card and we'll whizz one over to you.

Artist's impression. Is this what the box will look like?

bath birmingham brighton bristol cambridge cardiff edinburgh glasgow leeds liverpool london manchester nottingham oxford sheffield york

YOU'RE IN AN INTERVIEW

bath 2002

Welcome to Bath – the city that never sleeps... except for the eight hours after midnight or when it's just had one of those days. Packed with more listings and featuring more details than ever before, let itchy take you by the hand and lead you though the Georgian streets, giving you the lowdown on the best and the worst that the city has to offer.

So what else is different this year? Well the big news is the spa complex that opens in October. It promises to revitalize spa culture in the UK. Sadly we couldn't include it in the 2002 guide as when we went down to review it, we found nothing but a pile of breeze blocks, a couple of workman looking decidedly unbusy and a foreman who told us in no uncertain terms to um, stop trespassing. We left before he set his dog on us, but we'll be back. Look out for all the details on **www.itchybath.co.uk**

Another new development is the controversial experimental traffic system. If you plan to drive around the city this year, we have one word for you. Don't. The city is being redesigned to be more pedestrian-friendly, so leave your car at home and brave the streets on foot unless you fancy spending the day working on your anger management technique.

With more restaurants per square mile than London, a wealth of independent shops, some of the best drinking dens in the West Country and a club scene that rivals Stow-

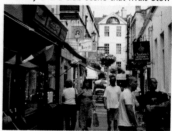

on-the-Wold on a Monday, you'll find all the old favourites as well as the newcomers reviewed here.

So what are you waiting for? Let itchy be your guide to all things entertainment, grab a bottle of Matey and jump on in.

DON'T GET INTIMIDATED BY THEIR EYE CONTACT

Two hours in Bath

Got your running shoes on? Right. First stop the Abbey. Push past the group of French students – yes, those guys with the multi-coloured clothes and matching backpacks who are marvelling at the amazing architecture. Take a few seconds to look then head out into the courtyard. Stop for a moment to watch the buskers performing. Half naked leather clad jugglers use this space often and will beg you to sign their petition. Do take the time to sign – Bath would be nothing without naked jugglers. Now look to your left – the Roman Baths. Don't bother with an audio guide. It's a hole in the ground filled with green slimy water, right? Cross the road and have a peek at the weir and before you is the famous Pulteney Bridge. After all this running around you need a drink. Peg it back to the Abbey where you'll spot the Crystal Palace tucked away down a side street. Then back to the station. Seen it, done it. Bought the t-shirt.

Two days in Bath – Expensive

Stay – It's got to be the Royal Crescent Hotel for the ultimate in blow out weekends; it's far from cheap with rooms starting from £100 per person, but hey, you deserve the best. Alternatively you could bring it down a notch or two and opt for the slightly more reasonable Francis Hotel in the very heart of the city – and with prices starting from just £70, it's a snip.

Shop – Easy. Stick to the top end of town and flash your cash in Shires Yard. Grab designer togs in Whistles, Square, Shoon or Jollys, buy your sarnies from Fodders and your household goods from The Alessi Gallery or Rossiters.

Attractions – Don't go mixing with the city low-life while you're here. You really should visit the Abbey and the Roman Baths – it's expected. But if you're looking for the ultimate Bath experience then you could take a champagne balloon flight and get a birds-eye view. The Costume Museum and The American Museum are certainly worth a look if you have time to spare, and don't forget to book a box at the Theatre Royal.

Eat – The ultimate is an evening meal at Lettonie, Bath's only restaurant with two Michelin stars. Failing that, make reservations at Le Clos, The Moody Goose or The Olive Tree. Alternatively you could visit Green Park Brasserie and enjoy live jazz and Anglo-French cuisine.

Drink – Join an older crowd at The Green Tree, The Star or the Ring O' Bells or settle for drinks at Bath's smallest pub, The Coeur de Lion. For the best cocktails in town, don't miss Pulp. If you fancy a quiet evening sipping champers then the upstairs bar at Browns is just the ticket.

Club – It's got to be Moles. There's really no other option. If money is no object then you might consider jumping in a cab and head-

"OI, WHAT ARE YOU LOT STARING AT!?"

ing for Bristol. The journey one-way will cost you around £16. Can't decide which Bristol club to visit? Treat yourself to itchy Bristol. Blatant self-promotion? Us? Never.

Alternatively, if you are set on staying in the city for a chilled Saturday night, The Fez isn't a bad bet.

Two days in Bath on a Budget

Accommodation – Bath Backpackers Hostel will be your first port of call. Failing that, get yourself bedded down at the YMCA. Both are central and very comfortable. More importantly, they're cheap.

Shop – Being skint doesn't exclude you from shopping. Well, that's what I tell my bank manager anyway. Check out Mrs. Simpson in Kingsmead Square for nearly new designer clobber, rummage through the bargain bin at Fat Face or treat yourself to a new toe-ring at Justice.

Attractions – Wanna bitta culture? The Victoria Art Gallery and The Hotbath Gallery are completely free to get into. Next, blag your way into the Roman Baths for free by pretending to be a Bath resident. Absolutely unmissable is a trip to Microworld. It's gonna set you back a couple of quid to get in but they promise to refund your money if you are not completely amazed. Try not to be completely amazed. It'll be difficult though, as the place is totally amazing.

Eat – Cheap nosh is everywhere in Bath. Your best bet is having the slap-up meal at lunchtime. Most restaurants offer an excellent lunchtime menu for up to 75% less than they charge in the evenings. Highly recommended cheap spots include Yum Yum Thai, Central Wine Bar, Bottelinos or Tilleys.

Drink – If you've got an NUS card then head for The Assembly, The Hobgoblin or Old Orleans. Stop off at The Litten Tree for a pint of Litten Ale – it'll cost you 99p. Otherwise head for The Hat and Feather, Belvedere Wine Vaults or The Porter.

Club – If you're skint then it doesn't really matter where you go as long as you get there early. If you wait until the pubs chuck out, you'll have to fork out more for door charges. Cadillacs serves the cheapest drinks of the lot of them though

Hotel £24, shopping £20, attractions £5, food £20, drink £25, club £5. **Total: £99**

So there you have it – a weekend in Bath with all the sights, a posh meal, a spot of shopping, a bit of culture, live music, a club and ten pints of lager for less than the price of four cocktails at The Mandarin Bar in London. Sorted.

BEWARE OF THE VOICES. FOR CAREER ADVICE WORTH LISTENING TO, INCLUDING **HELP** WITH **INTERVIEWS**, VISIT monster.co.uk

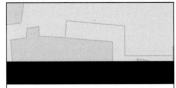

restaurants

www.itchybath.co.uk

■ ■ ■ American

■ ■ ■ California Kitchen
The Podium – (01225) 471471

Big open-plan restaurant with a customer base consisting of hordes of exhausted shoppers. It's not cheap, but the food's perfectly edible and it's not a bad place to stop off, particularly if you've just been shopping and need a few hours to formulate a plan. Yes, exactly how are you going to smuggle all those new clothes home without hubby finding out that you've been battering the Gold Card?

Sun-Fri 9.30-6. Sat 12.15-10
Meal for Two £28 (San Francisco lime chicken)

■ ■ ■ Firehouse Rotisserie
2 John Street – 482070

Although the menu isn't going to have Jamie Oliver quaking in his boots; it's fairly basic stuff, but done to a high standard. Pizza, lamb, chicken, steaks, there'll be something that takes your fancy. Caters well for big groups, especially those who appreciate a touch of style (it's quite plush inside), and for the cosy couples – don't panic – any rowdiness is usually confined to the function room upstairs. Great fun.

Mon-Fri 12-2.30 & 6-10.30, Sat 12-10.30
Meal for Two £38 (Rib steak)

■■■ Old Orleans
St Andrews Terrace, Bartlett Street
333233

Old Orleans. What image does that conjure up for you? Dark wooden panels and a sprinkling of neon 'Cocktails This Way' signs? Faded black and white photos of jazz greats? Popcorn dispensers? Jukeboxes? Yeah baby, this is tack-fest at its best, but hey, who cares when the drinks are cheap and the burgers are fat and chargrilled. A value eatery (and there ain't many of those in the city) attracting families, students and the odd grubby old man who can't afford to eat or drink anywhere else.
Mon-Sun 12-11
Meal for Two £36 (Surf 'n' Turf)

■■■ English

■■■ Browns
Orange Grove – 461199

Read any guidebook to Bath and they will tell you the history of Browns, waxing lyrical about the fact that it used to be a Magistrates Court, and they'll tell you that you simply must try and get seated at the back of the building where the cells used to be. Mmm, right. Let's set the record straight – police cells are not designed to create subtle ambience; they are designed as a place of punishment. Now Browns is a nice enough place, with decent grub and reasonable service but for gods sake don't let them seat you in the cells – they're awful.
Mon-Sun 12-11.30
Meal for Two £30 (Baked salmon)

■■■ Green Park Brasserie
Green Park Station – 338565

Housed in the original booking office of the station, this place is bright, spacious and friendly. The walls are used as exhibition space, given over to both local and internationally renowned artists, so the décor changes every time you visit. Anglo-French cuisine, the lunch menu is fairly simple, but the place really comes into its own in the evenings when it transforms into a venue for live jazz and the chef pulls out all the stops. Highly recommended.
Tue-Sun 10-10.30
Meal for Two £36 (Leg of lamb)

■■■ Hole in the Wall
George Street – 425242

What has happened to the Hole in the Wall? This used to be one of Bath's best restaurants, but it's hanging on by reputation alone. The quality of the food is certainly slipping, and although the setting is stunning, the fabulous décor won't take your mind off the fact that, for the price, the cuisine isn't quite up to scratch.
Mon-Sat 12-2.30 & 6-10
Meal for Two £40 (Pan fried fillet of seabass)

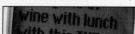

itchy sms @
www.itchybath.co.uk

▩▩■ Hullabaloos
Broad Street – 443323

Hullabaloos is a mad house. We mean that in a good way. The place attracts big crowds rather than quiet couples and the noise level reflects the restaurant's BYO policy. I mean, it's hard to stay silent when you're allowed to glug alcohol at supermarket prices. The food's cheap, cheerful and surprisingly tasty. Even veggies have no cause for complaint, as there's usually more to choose from than the ubiquitous vegetable lasagne. And if you run out of Strongbow Super, they may sell you more booze from their cellar.

Tue-Sat 12-2 & 6-11
Meal for Two £28 (Rack of lamb)

▩▩■ Lettonie
Kelston Road – 446676

This is the only restaurant in Bath with two Michelin stars. It's not in the centre so you'll need to grab a cab. And while you're at it, you'd better stop at the cashpoint – you're gonna need all the cash you can get if you plan to dine here. Posh – there's an understatement. Huge windows, fancy drapes, oil paintings and attentive service. The food's pretty damn good: French with a Latvian twist. Not the sort of place you'd go for a stag night, as diners tend to talk reverently in whispers. A gourmet's paradise.

Mon-Sun 12-2.30 & 7-10
Meal for Two £108 (Roast chicken)

▩▩■ The Moody Goose
Kingsmead Square – 466688

You wouldn't know that this place had been awarded a Michelin star. Not that the food's bad or anything – it's not. The food, the service and the whole dining experience are more than worthy of that accolade, but this place is just so un-up-itself. You can never be too over-dressed or under-dressed for the Moody Goose. The staff are superb and won't look down their noses at you if you can't make head nor tail of the menu. The restaurant area is non-smoking, but there's a small bar area that you can escape to if you're really gasping.

Mon-Sat 6-10.
Meal for Two £46 (Guinea fowl)

▩▩■ Moon and Sixpence
Broad Street – 460962

Locals frequently use this place as a wine bar, but the food is good too. Mostly English cuisine, but with a few surprises, there's a decent wine list and as the place isn't huge, a lively atmosphere even on slow nights. It's the perfect place for a romantic meal for two (or three?), but don't let them seat you upstairs – it's on the way to the bogs.

Mon-Sun 11.30-10.15
Meal For Two £38 (Loin of lamb)

LOOK AT HIM, POMPOUS IDIOT.

■ ■ ■ Olive Tree
Russell Street – 447928

Okay – this is so posh it's scary. Even if you can work out which knife goes with which course, you know you're going to make a total prat of yourself by knocking the wine bottle over, drinking out of the finger bowl or committing the cardinal sin of lighting up in this non-smoking restaurant. If you are prepared to brave the embarrassment or you're blessed with no pride or dignity whatsoever then you're in for one of the best meals you've ever tasted.

Mon-Sat 12.20-10.30, Sun 7-9
Meal for Two £52 (Lobster)

■ ■ ■ Sally Lunn's
North Parade Passage – 461634

Sally was a young French girl who arrived in Bath yonks ago, started making a brioche-style bread and was careless enough to lose the recipe. Years later, when she was dead and gone, renovations in the house uncovered her long lost recipe for this bread hidden behind a fireplace. A whole industry has sprung up based on her bread so if you're here in the daytime then grab a Sally Lunn bun and see what all the fuss is about. By night, the tea room transforms itself into an intimate (or cramped) dining room serving fairly standard cuisine to tourists. If Sally had only known how popular her little buns were going to be, she may have invested in a bigger house.

Mon-Sat 10-9, Sun 11-4
Meal for Two £23 (Breast of chicken)

■ ■ ■ Wife of Bath
Pierrepont Street – 461745

Hungry? I mean, really hungry? You're going to have to be if you intend to clear your plate here. Man-size portions and an eclectic menu featuring everything from bog standard lasagne to kangaroo meat. Full of everyone from Aussies to families to couples to students, the place appeals to all. It's light and spacious despite being a basement restaurant and the staff smile. We like it.

Mon-Sat 12-2.15 & 5.30-11, Sun 5-10
Meal for Two £32 (Medallions of kangaroo)

■ ■ ■ Woods
Alfred Street – 314812

Tucked away down a side street is this friendly little place, serving up Anglo-French cuisine in an unpretentious setting. There's a fair few veggie options for the leaf crunchers amongst you, and the service is faultless. Visit in the summer as they open this street up and throw a bit of a party, with live music, food, dancing and a beer tent. Recommended.

Mon-Sat 12-3 & 6-11, Sun 12-3
Meal For Two £40 (Barbary duck)

TOO BUSY DIGESTING HIS FOUR HOURS LUNCH TO LISTEN TO YOU

■ ■ ■ French

■ ■ ■ Le Beaujolais
Chapel Row – 423417

This little place has been going for years. It's become something of a favourite amongst the locals, offering decent French cooking in a very basic setting. The paper napkins and lack of trimmings are all supposed to be part of the charm, but it's bloody expensive to eat here and you'd think the least they could do is make linen napkins into fan shapes. Still, all the effort is concentrated on the food, and that's as it should be. If the weather's good, then head for the tables in the walled garden. Nice but pricey.

Mon-Thu 12-2.30 & 6-10, Fri 12-2.30 & 6-10.30, Sat 12-2.30 & 6-11
Meal for Two £42 (Seabass)

■ ■ ■ Café Rene
Shires Yard – 447147

Oui madame, je would like un petit taste of France. C'est possible to mange outside dans le courtyard? Oui? Fantasticament. Deux of your lovely baguettes s'il vous plait, and is that une yummy francais strawberry tarte that je see over there? Oui. Then donnez moi une of them and all please, they look bloody gorgeous. Café Rene is a great little French café-restaurant with outside seating in a little courtyard. Perfect for sunny summer lunches. Crap when it rains.

Mon-Sun 7-6
Meal for Two £22 (Ham baguette: we've assumed that you'd want wine with that)

■ ■ ■ Le Clos
Seven Dials – 444450

Formerly Le Clos du Roy, this place has changed name and management, but

thankfully the food hasn't changed a bit. Melt-in-your-mouth beef is always a treat and they cook it to perfection here. There's a pianist who tinkles away at the weekends and yes, it's formal, but the food is seriously good. If you weren't a foodie before you got here, you'll be converted. These guys have got French cuisine sorted. And I'm ashamed to say that us Brits cannot even hope to compete with the traditional roast they serve up on a Sunday. Where oh where is your Michelin star, Le Clos?

Mon-Sun 12-2.30 & 7-10
Meal for Two £36 (Veal)

WELL, DIGEST THIS!

■ ■ ■ Raphael
Upper Borough Walls – 480042

Ah, here's the new kid on the block. You can practically smell the paint as you walk through the door. It's early days for this place, but we're talking theatre-crowd here. Busy if there's something good on at the Royal, morgue-like if there's not. The food is reasonable French fare, but don't go asking to speak to Raphael – he doesn't exist. 'Why the name then?' we asked the owner, Luciano. 'Because it sounds French,' he replied. Right, well that's cleared that up then.

Mon-Sat 11-3 & 5.30-11, Sun 11-3 & 5.30-10
Meal for Two £33 (Entrecote Raphael)

■ ■ ■ Tilleys
North Parade Passage – 484200

A real favourite with the locals. Rather than choosing a main course, you just order starter portions. You can then eat as much or as little as you like. Perfect for couples, big groups, singletons and, well, anyone really. Friendly atmosphere, efficient service, great food...stop me if I'm gushing.

Mon-Sat 12-2.30 & 6.30-11
Meal for Two £26 (Venison rissoles)

■ ■ ■ Indian

■ ■ ■ Eastern Eye
Quiet Street – 422323

It's the end of the night and you're gagging for a curry. Fourteen pints of lager are starting to pick a hole in your stomach lining and you just need that biryani to set the whole

vomiting process off. Don't even try this place; it's not the one for you at all. This is Indian cuisine at its finest. The restaurant itself is pretty impressive, with ornate Georgian ceilings and a spacious dining area. There's no swirly carpets to puke on and no burgundy curtains to blow your nose on so, like I said, this is not the place to come after a night on the booze. Superior Indian cuisine in a fabulous setting and service to match.

Sun-Thu 12-2.30 & 6-11
Fri-Sat 12-2.30 & 6-11.30.
Meal for Two £33 (Prawn jalfrezi)

■ ■ ■ Jamuna
9 High Street – 464631

Reckon you can make the stairs? Go on mate, you go ahead of me and I'll catch you if you fall. Just around the corner from All Bar One, you'll find this brightly lit curry house. The chef has won awards for his fine Indian cuisine, but who gives a toss when it's ten past eleven and you've got a craving for a tikka masala. Just got to make it up those stairs first.

Mon-Sun 12-2.30 & 6-12
Meal for Two £31 (Tandoori platter)

BEWARE OF THE VOICES. FOR CAREER ADVICE WORTH LISTENING TO,
INCLUDING HELP WITH INTERVIEWS, VISIT monster.co.uk

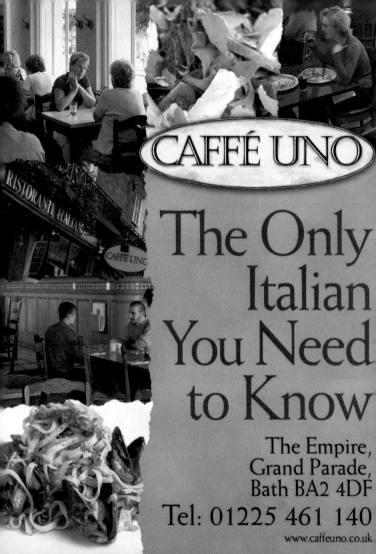

CAFFÉ UNO

The Only
Italian
You Need
to Know

The Empire,
Grand Parade,
Bath BA2 4DF
Tel: 01225 461 140
www.caffeuno.co.uk

■■■ Rajpoot

Argyle Street – 466833

Okay – this place is pretty damn cool. There's a little doorman who invites you in to 'sample the tastes of India'. Inside, it's a proper restaurant. None of your burgundy flock wallpaper and pictures of tigers in here. A regular winner of Indian Restaurant of The Year means that we're talking top notch curries here. But at a price – it ain't cheap.

Sun-Wed 6-1.30, Thu-Sat 6-2
Meal for Two £28 (Tandoori chicken + rice)

■■■ Italian

■■■ Ask

Broad Street – 789997

Be afraid. Be very afraid. Never in my life have I come so close to screaming in a restaurant as I did when I visited here. It wasn't the food that caused such distress; the pasta and pizza dishes are pretty good. It wasn't the décor; bright coloured sofas to doss on while you're waiting and a well-lit dining area with stone floors. Nor was it the wine list; that's reasonable too. It's the bloody mannequin that stands by the entrance. I believe it's supposed to resemble a friendly waiter, but I have a sneaking suspicion that The London Dungeon is missing an exhibit.

Mon-Sun 12-11
Meal for Two £24 (Fusilli al rustica)

■■■ Bella Pasta

Milsom Street – 462368

Food like mama used to make. That's assuming that mama was a trash-junkie with a bitch of a hangover and no culinary skills whatsoever. This place seems to rely on ignorant tourists and eighteen-year old Bathonians who wouldn't know good Italian if it jumped up and smacked 'em in the tastebuds.

Mon-Wed 10-10, Thu-Sat 10-11, Sun 12-10
Meal for Two £29 (Smokey spaghetti)

■■■ Bottelinos

Bladud Buildings – 464861

Ever wondered what's at the bottom of a beer barrel? Wanna find out? Head to Bottelinos; they've lodged a beer barrel in between the floors and created a downstairs viewing gallery. itchy loves Bottelinos. It's big, with stacks of seating. It's crowded, with large groups and romantic couples. It's cheap, with pizzas starting at just £6; they're tasty, and so are the waiters. Fast, friendly service, banisters cunningly disguised as barber poles, and best of all, the wine comes in huge carafes. Brilliant.

Mon-Sat 12-2.30 & 5.30-11, Sun 5.30-11
Meal for Two £23 (Penne Arrabbiata)

■■■ Caffe Uno

Grand Parade – 461140

You'll not find a more impressive setting for gorging on pasta than this one. The restaurant is part of the Empire building and boasts frescoes on the walls, waiters that won't spit in your food and a long and confusing wine list to study intently before plumping for the house white.

Sun-Thu 9.30-10.30, Fri-Sat 9.30-11
Meal for Two £25 (Gnocchi Modena)

■ ■ ■ Capetti's
Argyle Street – 442299

Cheap, cheerful and serving up some of the best Italian food in the city. This is the sort of place where diners chat across the tables, where there's always someone having some sort of birthday celebration, where the staff actually look pleased to see you and where the chef has actually mastered the art of cooking. And if you stray from the usual pizza-pasta chains and check it out, you'll be pleased to discover that there's also the bonus of an atmosphere. One to check out.
Tue-Sat 12-2 & 6.30-10.30
Meal for Two £34 (Bistella al Pepe)

■ ■ ■ Pizza Express
Barton Street – 420119

Watch the lads in embarrassing black and white striped uniforms cook your pizza in full view. Comment loudly on how degrading it must be to actually have to wear those outfits in public. Laugh at the silly hats they are forced to wear before digging into the usual Pizza Express favourites. It's worth dining here just for the smug feeling you get; better still, that feeling will last for hours and hours – or at least until you have to go home

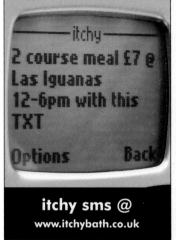

itchy sms @
www.itchybath.co.uk

to get into your green-striped dungarees and baseball cap and head off for another hard days graft at the local DIY store.
Mon-Sun 12-11
Meal for Two £24 (Soho pizza)

■ ■ ■ Oriental

■ ■ ■ Chopstick
Southgate – 425067

Get the decorators in. Please. If I have to stare at those gaudy red walls one more time, I swear I'll stab someone with my chopsticks. If I hate it so much, why not eat elsewhere? 'Cos Chopstick serves up the best sweet and sour chicken in the city at half the price of the other restaurants. That's why. Don your dark glasses and pay a visit.
Mon-Sat 12-2 & 6-11.30
Meal for Two £27 (Sweet and sour fish)

■■■ Peking

Kingsmead Square – 466377

This is a posh restaurant full of romantic couples enjoying the superior cuisine. It's enough to make you sick – the lovey-dovey couples I mean, not the food. The food's bloody good and there's lots of it, but it's not one for singletons or groups. The seafood is especially good here so I'm destined to return again and again and dine on fine Chinese cuisine while I wait for my social life to pick up.

Mon-Sun 12-2 & 6-11.15
Meal for Two £34 (Fried squid)

■■■ Xian

Charles Street – 424917

This place is stuck slightly out of the way, so you're usually guaranteed a table. It's a shame really, as the place serves up great Chinese and the restaurant area is far nicer than the exterior would lead you to believe. It's fairly small inside, but if you're drunk enough you can kid yourself it's bigger by being fooled by the mirrored walls. Definitely worthy of closer inspection.

Tue-Sat 12-2 & 6.30-11, Sun-Mon 6.30-11
Meal for Two £29 (Crispy duck)

■■■ Yum Yum Thai

Kingsmead Square – 445253

Not one to visit with even a vaguely ugly dining partner as this place is brighter than the inside of the sun. However, the food is great, cheap and plentiful. The service is friendly and the waitresses giggle a lot; this is either charming or annoying depending on whether you are a happy-go-lucky type or a miserable sod. Good value Thai lunches.

Mon-Sun 11-11
Meal for Two £26 (Kang Daeng Kai)

■■■ Vegetarian

■■■ Demuth's

North Parade Passage – 446059

Rabbit food for the namby-pamby vegetarian brigade? Get yourself a nice rare steak folks, you'll feel so much better for it. If vege-

tarian cuisine can be tasty and filling, I'll eat my hat. Famous last words. After they'd finished battering me (and those vegetarian folk are stronger than they look) they took me up on this challenge and I have to confess that the food here is enough to convert any hardened carnivore overnight. That's not to say that I am a die-hard vegan now; I've still got half a trilby to get through before I'm allowed back. Excellent vegan and vegetarian cuisine, efficient service and a decent wine list makes this an itchy favourite.

Sun-Fri 10-5.30 & 6-10; Sat 9-5.30 & 6-11
Meal for Two £22 (Goat's cheese and pesto organic bagel)

■■■ Porter Bar

George Street – 424104

Yes, we know it isn't really a restaurant, but it's hard enough to find vegetarian places at the best of times and this one fits the bill. It's Bath's only vegetarian pub so expect to find lots of worthy people saving whales, signing petitions and digging into vegetarian pub grub. Actually, it's a great little place with pretty standard fare, and prices that won't break the bank. Great value.

Mon-Sun 11-9
Meal for Two £19 (Cashew nut curry)

■ ■ ■ Walrus and Carpenter
Barton Street – 314864

Just up from the Theatre Royal, this place is an absolute homely gem. Inside there's a series of tiny rooms over three floors, with just a couple of tables squeezed into each. The food's not strictly vegetarian and they do a nice line in burgers, but the menu has a strong vegetarian slant and most non-meat eaters in the area will list this place as one of their favourites. Better still, you can wash the lot down with some Walrus cocktails. Highly recommended.

Mon-Sat 12-1.30 & 6-11, Sun 12-11
Meal for Two £29 (Walrus seafood bake)

■ ■ ■ Seafood

■ ■ ■ Green Street Seafood Café
Green Street – 448707

Light, bright and stinking of fish, The Good Food Guide raves about this place, and we have to admit, it's pretty damn good. It's on top of the fish market so the food couldn't be any fresher. A definite winner.

Tue-Sat 12-2 & 6-10.30
Meal for Two £34 (Cornish crab with tarragon mayonnaise)

■ ■ ■ Loch Fyne Restaurant
Milsom Street – 750120

This is a strange one. It's far from cheap, and situated in what used to be a bank. There are high Georgian ceilings and a gorgeous outlook, but the restaurant is laid out like a school canteen. Tables in rows and servers at the top of the restaurant. You almost expect the headmaster to come in, cough loudly, and tell everyone to keep the noise down a bit. It shouldn't work, but it does. What's their secret? Well it seems that good seafood is hard to come by, and this place does seafood well. Most of the fish come from Loch Fyne, so they are responsibly farmed in a pollution-free environment. And they even serve breakfasts seven days a week so you can pop in for kippers, toast and tea for less than £6.

Mon-Thu 9-10, Fri-Sat 9-11, Sun 10-10
Meal for Two £54 (Seafood platter)

■ ■ ■ Seafoods Fish and Chips
Kingsmead Square – 465190

Licensed fish and chip shop. Battered cod, scampi...you name it, they'll deep fry it and open a nice (and I use that word advisedly) bottle of wine to go with it. Best avoided on Wednesday lunchtime when the place fills up with old biddies taking advantage of the 'senior citizens special'. Nothing like the smell of urine-soaked pantyhose to put you off your dinner.

Mon-Sat 11.30-11.30, Sun 12-9
Meal for Two £18 (Cod & chips)

PC 975 O'Hagan, 50(ish), policeman

We all know members of the constabulary like a drink, where? Baty's

Not while you're on duty, I'm sure.

Where do you eat? Any Indian or Italian – they're all great.

Where do you... Not anymore, I don't.

Where do you go shopping? HMV

Fun lovin' Criminals or The Police I suppose. What's best about Bath? The people

They can't all be criminals, what's the worst? Damn seagulls.

■ ■ ■ World Cuisine

■ ■ ■ La Flamenca
North Parade – 463626

Can't afford a holiday this year? Even a fortnight in Bognor is out of your price range? Fret not. Get yourself down to this little gem (sorry for the cliché, but it really is) for authentic Spanish cuisine, and better still, live music and flamenco dancers to enhance your eating experience at the weekend. Paella is highly recommended, though the tapas is equally popular. And the chef is the most beautiful man I have ever laid...where was I? Oh yes...my eyes on.

Mon-Sat 12-3 & 6.30-12
Meal for Two £30 (Paella)

■ ■ ■ Las Iguanas
Seven Dials – 336666

Oh baby, take me away from this stuffy Georgian city and transport me to Latin America. I need to feel love in my food. I want

bright coloured walls and crazy lights on the ceilings. I want to eat tapas by day and XimXim by night. I want to stay up late while beautiful senoritas bring me tequila...and so here it is. Cracking little restaurant serving lethal cocktails and decent Sunday hangover breakfasts.

Mon-Thu 12-11, Fri-Sat 12-11.30, Sun 12-10.30. Meal for Two £27 (XimXim – Brazilian lime chicken)

■ ■ ■ Sands
George Street – 443900

Lebanese cuisine in a pretty posh environment. Situated in historic Edgar Buildings, Sands gives you high ceilings, chandeliers, hookahs and lots of white linen as well as the best, and uh only, Lebanese food in the city. If you're looking to dine on Lebanese then this is the place to be. If you're looking to dine on French, then it isn't. Simple.

Mon-Sun 12-2 & 6-11
Meal for Two £33 (Suyahdiyah)

!	🗋 🖉	From	Subject
	✉	itchycity.co.uk	Restaurant recommendations via e-mail

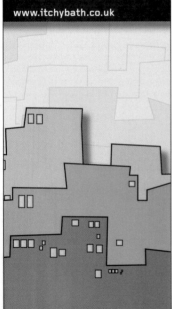

■ ■ ■ All Bar One
High Street – (01225) 324021

You know the score by now. Seen one – seen 'em all. There's the usual selection of wines and beers, the usual good quality food and the Bath branch is handily situated in the centre of the city so it's a great place to stop for a spot of lunch with friends. Absolutely packed at the weekends, as good a place as any to go with a large crowd, but with huge windows the length of the building it's not the best spot for any kind of intimacy. Planning to seduce your best mate's bird over a glass or two of bubbly? Best grab a seat at the back then. Take it from one who knows and still has the bruises to show for it. Over 21s only.

Mon-Sun 11-11
Cheeseburger and fries £3.95

■ ■ ■ Bar Karanga
Manvers Street – 446545

Most bars are found at the top end of town, but Bar Karanga has flouted tradition and sits at the bottom, just a stagger away from the train station. It's a decent sized place with bright décor, comfortable seating and friendly staff, but it has suffered somewhat from a lack of decent clientele. Weekends see stag parties from Bristol falling off the train and into the bar, but on the whole the alcopop brigade rule here, so expect lots of pretty young things dressed up to the nines in mum's high heels, trying desperately to appear old enough to smoke. Of course, if that's your thing then you'll be in paradise. Just remember that the cop shop is directly across the road and that the age of consent is sixteen, and you'll be fine.

Mon-Fri 4-11, Sat 2-11

A MELLOW MIX OF SPIRIT AND SOUL.
THAT FLAVOURS WHATEVER IT TOUCHES.

FEEL THE PRESENCE

TREVOR NELSON. DJ

Try it with soda and ice in a wild club.

Baty's
George Street - 331532

If you're under thirty then you're too young. It's a popular spot for the fashionably-challenged. Everyone in Baty's thinks they're incredibly cool and 'on the pulse'. They aren't, of course, but it's nice that they have found a little spot in the city where they can enjoy a drink and pretend to be far more popular/successful/loaded (delete as applicable) than they actually are. If Bath had a New Media crowd, then this is where they'd set up base.
Mon-Sat 11-11, Sun 12-10.30
Pasta carbonara £6.75

Browns
Orange Grove – 461199

While the rest of the city bars are heaving and there's a half hour queue to reach the bar, Browns manages to keep the crowds at bay. If you fancy a quiet evening dossing on squidgy sofas and actually want to be able to hear what your date is talking about (why would you want to do that?) then head for the upstairs bar. And if you're feeling peckish there's usually tables in the restaurant.
Mon-Sun 12-11.30
Baked salmon £9.95

Central Wine Bar
Upper Borough Walls – 333939

Recently refurbished, Central is now bigger and better than it was before. Don't be too concerned though, the new look Central hasn't lost any of its charm in the re-fit. You can still find a decent selection of bottled and draught beer, thirteen wines by the glass and fantastic, yet reasonably priced, food. Most importantly, they haven't done away with the genuinely friendly welcome or the table service. The place where everybody knows your name, this is Cheers, but with classy décor and a funkier Sam Malone. Excellent staff and 40% bigger measures on spirits. What can I say? It's a winner.
Mon-Sun 12-11 (Food: Mon-Sat 12-6, Sun 12-4)
Homemade salmon fishcake £5.95

Lambretta's
North Parade House – 464650

Oh dear. Oh dear. Oh dear. Somebody tell me that I haven't just spotted a bloke in a 'Frankie Says' T-shirt. I think I need to go and have a lie down now. If you can disregard the fashion sense (or lack of it) of some of the clientele, Lambretta's is the ideal place to go if you're planning a night out at Po Na Na's, which is just next door. Grab a window seat and you can keep one eye on the queue, the other on the retro décor and try to forget the fact that this place is flypaper for freaks.
Mon-Sat 12-11, Sun 12-10.30
Cheese toastie £2.50

■ ■ ■ Litten Tree
Milsom Street - 310772

The interior decorators were a brave lot here. They've taken a historical building, filled it with fake pillars and tried to pass it off as a pre-club bar. Actually, it works. We're not sure how, but it does. There's a huge sports screen showing all the big matches and great deals on food and drinks. It's a decent place to stop off for a spot of lunch. By night the Litten Tree becomes a lively venue, attracting a young crowd with some enormous bouncers to keep watch on the door. On Thursdays all drinks are £1.50 and Litten Ale, their own brew, is just 99p a pint. And if, like the rest of us, you've noticed that Bath isn't falling over itself with excellent clubs then you can get a ticket to The Works in Bristol on Saturdays; it's £6 and includes return transport and entry.
Mon-Sat 11-11, Sun 11-10.30 (Food served until 9)
Red Thai curry £5.50

■ ■ ■ Mothers
St James Parade - 318200

It's official: there are no more bars anymore. There's café-bars, restaurant-bars, iron bars, but what happened to all those bars that were just bars? Mothers is, according to the blurb, a restaurant-bar-place. A 21st century label for a 21st century restaurant-bar-place. Think swanky London bar. Think desperately uncomfortable seating. Think the owner should probably move location and he'd make a killing. Paying a fortune for drinks and poncing around in shoes that make your feet bleed doesn't automatically make for a great night out. Saying that, there's always a few tourists from the Smoke who think it's the bees knees; you certainly won't find many of the local yokels supping at the bar. Second home to the beautiful people and the wannabe beautiful people, though to be fair, it does have some beautiful bog seats, so the toilets are certainly worth checking out.
Mon-Sat 11-11, Sun 12-10.30 (Food served Mon-Sat12-2.30, 6-11; Sun 6-10.30)
Seared calves' livers £8

■ ■ ■ Old Orleans
St. Andrews Terrace, Bartlett St - 333233

Not a bad little spot for cheap grub during the day, but Old Orleans comes into its own in the evenings. Special offers on cocktails during the week bring in the students and impoverished youth of Bath. Tip: flash your NUS card rather than your cash for 20% off your total bill. You can even get yourself plastered on bottled beers here on a

A **MELLOW** MIX OF SPIRIT AND SOUL.
THAT FLAVOURS **WHATEVER IT TOUCHES.**

Thursday night for just a quid a throw. Unsurprisingly, there are more than a few students falling off stools at the end of the night. But that's a plus.

Mon-Sun 12-11
Surf 'n' Turf £12.25

■ ■ Pulp
Monmouth Street – 466411

Forget all your preconceptions. Cocktails aren't just for ponced-up media prats with more money than sense. James 'Turbo' Timothy, creator of the famous Chocolate Monkey, brings cocktails to the masses and he does it with style. Gasp with amazement as he explains the difference between a slurpy and a sour. Shriek with delight as he swings his bottle opener. Shake your head sadly as he explains how Hollywood has failed to recognise his many talents. But Hollywood's loss is our gain. Turbo has made the bar his stage and, as a leading man, he rocks. A true visionary, Turbo was the first of the cocktail kings to include peanut butter in one of his drinks. They said he was mad. They may have been right. But itchy loves him anyway, and he can certainly knock up

the best Manhattan this side of...erm...Manhattan, or London even. Quality stuff. If you only have one night in Bath then you should be spending it here.

Mon-Sat 11-11, Sun 12-10.30 (Finger food only served after 7.30)
Brie and vegetable stack - £6.50, Nachos - £4, Slurpies - £3.90

■ ■ Raincheck Bar
Monmouth Street – 444770

Ever wondered where the ladies who lunch go in the evenings? They all hot-foot it down to The Raincheck to sample the many charms of the host, Mark. Table service, outside seating, decent food, great cocktails, and possibly the best coffee in the city keep them coming back. Attracting an older crowd, it's a relaxed and friendly little spot to meet up with friends on a summer evening before heading to the theatre.

Mon-Sat 10-11, Sun 11.30-10
Tiger prawns £6.40

■ ■ Ring O' Bells
Widcombe Parade – 448870

If you like jazz in a friendly atmosphere, you'll love the Ring O' Bells. Laid-back, unpretentious and with excellent food to boot, the Ring O' Bells attracts an older crowd so no young hoolies to ruin your evenings here. A decent selection of real ales and an innovative menu, it's just a shame you get kicked out at 11. Yet another crap statistic of the archaic Bath licensing laws.

Mon-Sat 12-11, Sun 12-10.30
Sunday roast £5

■■■ RSVP

Edgar Buildings – 789050

Being a bit of a lazy git, I popped into RSVP, pushed the snogging couple from the sofa, ordered meself a nice G&T and handed my pen over to the regulars of RSVP and demanded that they review the place themselves. They said: Packed. Crammed. Stuffy. Good. Busy. Big. They sell drinks. Sometimes they do cheap drinks but not always. Just like really good. There's a fair bit of talent. The sort of place that you know...it's just good. So there you have it. Proof, if any were needed, that RSVP is good. Proof, if any were needed, that you should never trust pissed-up people to write reviews.

Mon-Sat 8am-11pm, Sun 10-10.30 (Food served till 9)

Sausage and mash - £4.95

itchy sms @
www.itchybath.co.uk

■■■ Shades

Edgar Buildings – 466667

Low ceilings make this a real hazard area for tall folk who've had too much vodka. There's not a lot of them about in Shades (probably got concussed on their first visit) and so shorties rule here. This is a great little bar-restaurant or restaurant-bar, but the real bonus here is the fabulous garden area. If the weather's fine then it's fairly unbeatable. If it's raining or you're in the mood for lurrvvve then you'll be well impressed with the candlelit tables in the main restaurant area.

Mon-Sun 12-11, Sun 12-10.30 (Food served: Mon-Fri 12-2, Sat 12-5, Mon-Thu 6-9)

Lasagne with salad £5.10

■■■ Slug and Lettuce

George Street – 337666

A popular spot at the top of town with excellent bar staff and some great furniture. Look out for the wibbly shaped tables; they have a raised lip so you can fill them up with beer, make little boats out of crisp packets and sail them across the table towards your friends. If you are far too grown up for such immature pursuits then there's table football to take your mind off the prices; £2.75 for a pint of lager – if I wanted to pay London prices I'd go to London.

Mon-Sun 12-11 (Food served until 9pm)

Avocado ciabatta sandwich £4.75

MORGAN'S SPICED

A MELLOW MIX OF SPIRIT AND SOUL THAT FLAVOURS WHATEVER IT TOUCHES.

pubspubspubspubspubspubspubspubspubspubspubspubspubs

www.itchybath.co.uk

■ ■ ■ Assembly Inn
16-17 Alfred Street – (01225) 333639
Handily placed just minutes from the Costume Museum and Assembly Rooms, this recently refurbished pub attracts a mixed bag of tourists and poverty-stricken students who take advantage of the cheap booze. With big windows lining the walls of both bars, a pool table and a TV inevitably tuned to the latest match, it's not a bad place to stop for a pint or two.
Food: 12-7 Mon-Sun

■ ■ ■ The Beehive
3 The Belvedere, Lansdown Road – 420274
Not the smartest pub in Bath by a long shot, but if you're prepared to hike for your pint then join the swarm of other cider drinkers at the Beehive. They all made the trip, have built their own community and now only need to come out for the dole cheque run. Feeling peckish? Well they may just rustle you up a bag of crisps or a pickled egg if you're lucky.

■ ■ ■ The Bell
103 Walcot Street – 460246
Sister pub to the Hat and Feather, this place is the biz if you're looking for wall-to-wall humanity. There's an outside courtyard that gets seriously packed in summer, live music three times a week, rickshaws out the back, a dartboard, games room, chess and a bar billiards table. The perfect place to sample some unusual ale and start philosophical debates on whether herpes is worse than income tax.

■ ■ ■ The Belvedere Wine Vaults
25 Belevedere, Lansdown Road – 330264
The night starts here and if you're not careful it'll end here too; it's hard to pull yourself

away. This is a cracking little place that suffers somewhat from being stuck halfway up Lansdown Hill, so tourists only find it if they get lost. Get there early (you won't be able to face the hike later) and pay no attention to the outside (it's cleverly disguised as a place that thrives on the domino-player trade) and check out one of the friendliest pubs in the city. There's a decent selection of real ales and live music most nights provided by whoever brings their guitar.

Food 12-9 Mon-Sun

■ ■ ■ The Boater
9 Argyle Street – 464211

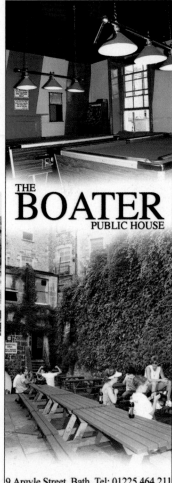

The Boater is the only city pub that can boast a riverside (well, almost) setting. In the summer, make your way to the beer garden and enjoy splendid views of the weir. Be warned: the place gets seriously packed when Bath Rugby is playing at home, but if you can squeeze past the sports fans it's well worth stopping for a while. There's a pool table, sports screen and a cellar bar along with good food and good company of all ages and inclinations.

Food 12-3 Mon-Sun

9 Argyle Street, Bath, Tel: 01225 464 211

20

■ ■ ■ The Brain Surgery
36-37 Dafford Street – 330056

Ever watched The League of Gentlemen? Well, this is a local pub for local people – there's nothing for you here. Of course, if you haven't watched The League of Gentlemen then I should add that there's a pool table, a couple of dartboards and a selection of ales from Wales. This pub would be quite at home in Royston Vassey. You've been warned.
Food 12-7 Mon-Sun

■ ■ ■ The Crystal Palace
Abbey Green – 424210

At between three hundred and four hundred years old, this is a place with history – and its own ghost, if the stories are to be believed. However, the only spirits that caught my eye where the ones behind the bar. Bright and spacious with two bars, a conservatory and a heated courtyard complete with fountain and vine-covered gazebo, you'd expect to be paying through the nose. You'd be wrong. Despite being right in the centre of the city, they serve cocktails and shooters at out-of-town prices (cocktails from £2.75, shooters from £2). Clientele range from tourists to a more sedate twenty-something professionals and rather sensible student types. Perfect for a quiet drink.
Food 12-8.30 Mon-Sun

■ ■ ■ Coeur de Lion
Northumberland Place – 463568

The Coeur de Lion has no option but to offer seating outside all year round. It's a busy place and inside there's not enough room to swing even the tiniest of kittens. It's Bath's smallest pub and as such, a total tourist magnet. Don't let that put you off though – it really is worth squeezing through the doors and checking it out. A selection of newspapers, friendly staff, a couple of board games, flowers on the tables and excellent bar meals served, mean that this place ranks amongst most local's top five drinking dens. Size isn't everything, right lads?
Food 12-2.30 Mon-Sun

top 5 for...
Playing Pool

1. Porter Bar
2. Smith Brothers
3. The Huntsman
4. The Hat and Feather
5. Savilles

couple of nights a week, which is a blessing or a nightmare depending on whether the bloke in front of the mike can actually sing. Bar food is served weekday lunchtimes but there's a shop next door that sells pasties if you are hungry outside these hours, and as long as you keep your pint topped up the landlord doesn't complain if you bring your own.

Food 12-2.30 Mon-Fri

■ ■ ■ The Farmhouse
Lansdown Road – 316162

Without the music, this'd be a pretty ordinary place. The landlord knows this and has taken steps to remedy the situation. The Farmhouse has earned itself the reputation of best live jazz venue in the city. Four nights a week, top local musicians play their hearts out to adoring crowds. If you prefer to be able to hear what the person next to you is saying then you can take a seat around the corner where you won't have to resort to sign language to communicate. Don't head back down the hill without checking out the neighbouring Camden Crescent – it's the only unfinished crescent in the city and affords some amazing views for the sober and not so sober.

■ ■ ■ First Inn Last Out
1 Beaufort West, London Road – 425786

Chrome, mirrors and a bit of a 1930's feel – Filos is a popular no nonsense pub. There's a couple of screens inevitably tuned to the sports channel, a pool table, darts, and the occasional live band. There's also karaoke a

■ ■ ■ The Grapes
14 Westgate Street – 310235

Many an unsuspecting tourist has been lured inside by the cheap (and sometimes even free) drinks. Small and dingy, you'll find a full quota of old codgers propping up the bar. Girls – word of advice; leave your short skirts behind, the crumblies get more than a little excited by a glimpse of a well turned ankle and you'll be fighting the regulars off all night. Bar meals are cheap and cheerful, but best avoided unless you have the constitution of a concrete elephant.

Food 12-2.30 Mon-Sat

MORGAN'S SPICED

A MELLOW MIX OF SPIRIT AND SOUL. THAT FLAVOURS WHATEVER IT TOUCHES.

Gay Pubs

OK, so it's not exclusively gay, but the **Dark Horse** on 4 Northampton Street (425944) is gay friendly. A regular kind of pub, nothing special – nonetheless, a nice enough mixed lez and gay hang out.

Then, there's the **Bath Tap**, on 19 St James Parade (404344). Bath's official gay venue. Bright, cheerful and tongue-in-cheek, The Bath Tap hosts everything from regular 60s nights to karaoke, as well as the excellent Drag Night Quiz on a Wednesday. There's a function room for fetish nights and parties, and they've wangled a late licence on Fridays and Saturdays so you won't have to drag yourself away 'til 2am. Music – chart and cheese, mostly.

Then there's the **Garrick's Head**, on 8 St John's Place (318368) – more gay-friendly than gay, but then so is every other pub in Bath. Perhaps it's because of the location; The Garricks Head is situated next door to the Theatre Royal and does attract more thespians than most. It's a great little place, light and bright inside with friendly staff, funky music and outside seating – ideally placed for the national sport of people-watching. gay.uk.net

■ ■ ■ Hat and Feather
14 London Street – 425672

No visit to Bath is complete without taking at least one drink at The Hat. You won't be able to stop at one. You know that and I

know that, and so does da management. This pub is seriously packed every night of the week. It's a strange old place with a rigorous line-up of entertainment, but if you're in the city during the week then you have to get down there on a Wednesday and catch DJ Derek. The guy is a local legend. This is Bath entertainment at its best. And while you're there, check out the wild display on the ceiling. With a pool table upstairs, a bohemian crowd and great music, it's a fantastic place to get totally wasted.

■ ■ ■ Hatchetts
7 Queen Street – 425045

This place looks a bit 'spit and sawdust': real ales, wine that tastes like vinegar, crap furniture and an enormous embroidery of a Honda Gold Wing taking pride of place on the wall. In reality, Hatchetts is full of estate agents and computer technicians who shrug off the suits and sling on the leathers and play at being hard men and bikers for the night before rushing home to check if mummy has ironed their shirt for the morning. Girls; take your pick – if you're looking to pull a forty-year old virgin then you've come to the right place. Inverted pretension at its very worst. But I guess anywhere that keeps these twats away from the general public can't be all bad.

■ ■ ■ The Hobgoblin
47 St James's Parade – 460785

You are allowed in here without a NUS card, but best beg, borrow or steal one anyway and get yourself 20% discount on drinks every afternoon. But that's not the only rea-

Colette, 25, tourist

OK so without this book where would you drink? The Pig & Fiddle
And grub? The Walrus & Carpenter
Where are you planning to get down? Moles
Where are you spending your pocket money? Jack 'n' Danny's and Shoon.
What's the best thing about Bath? Loads of festivals
And the worst? I've got to go home tomorrow.

son that The Hobgoblin is popular with the students. There's a decent choice of real ales – including Hobgoblin and Wychwood Special, music loud enough to burst eardrums, over 30 flavoured vodkas and the occasional live band. Hungry? Choose from standard ploughmans and burgers or treat yourself to the epitome of English cuisine, the deep-fried Mars Bar.

Food 12-2.30 Mon-Wed, 12-5 Thu-Fri, 12-4 Sat-Sun

■ ■ ■ The Huntsman

Terrace Walk – 482900

Handily situated opposite Bog Island – this is one of the few places in Bath that you can get a drink until 2am, six days a week. There's a couple of pool tables and a dancefloor, should you fancy the exercise. Crowded with late-night drinkers most nights of the week, you'd assume that this would be an excellent place to pull. Not so. Sadly the words 'beautiful' and 'people' do not come to mind when describing the clientele; 'nuclear' and 'disaster' would be more appropriate – with fashion sense to match. Still, they're an up-for-it crowd if you're not fussy. And after a couple more pints, some of them may even look quite appealing.

Food 12-8.30 Mon-Sat, 12-5 Sun

■ ■ ■ Lamb and Lion

Lower Borough Walls – 474931

An excellent pre-club stop-off. At weekends it's standing room only and packed with tartlets who desert the place at 10pm to get cheap admission to the clubs. Word of warning though – when they say they close at 11pm, they ain't joking; short of physically picking you up and flinging you onto the streets they'll do anything to get you out before last orders, even locking the toilets at 10.30pm to deter stragglers.

Food 12-5 Mon-Sun

A MELLOW MIX OF SPIRIT AND SOUL THAT FLAVOURS WHATEVER IT TOUCHES.

■ ■ ■ Old Green Tree

Green Street – 448259

There's three tiny rooms: the front room, the standing room, and the non-smoking room. Real ales are served by attractive barmaids and they host the occasional jazz/blues night or art exhibition. Food is served at lunchtimes only – it's not the cheapest in the city but it's not your standard pub grub either.

Food 12-3 Mon-Sun

· ■ ■ The Oliver

Green Street – 464666

The Oliver is famed for being home of the Bath Oliver biscuit. Nobody in the pub could explain this claim to my satisfaction, so exactly why the biscuit needed a home remains a mystery. The aforementioned biscuit was actually developed by Dr. William Oliver as a remedy for indigestion. The biscuits are still made today and sold as a delicacy – though not in this pub, as it happens. And quite rightly so – pubs sell beer not biscuits.

■ ■ ■ Pig and Fiddle

2 Saracen Street – 460868

Bathonians love The Pig. It's great. Not as tatty as a pub, not as try-hard trendy as a bar, The Pig sits happily in the middle and is popular with students, twenty-somethings and ageing hippies. Everyone's happy. Big outside seating area with benches spilling out onto the street just perfect for inhaling traffic fumes in the summer. Sadly it falls prey to the office-party dickheads in the winter. Visit in December and you'll inevitably find Nigel from accounts prancing around in santa earmuffs that were oh so funny for the first five minutes. The regulars desert the place over Christmas and regain control of this brilliant little watering hole in January safe in the

knowledge that Nigel and his ilk will not be allowed out for another twelve months.

Food 12-6 Mon-Sun

■ ■ ■ The Porter

15 George Street – 424104

Don't go there. Stay away. That's what the regulars asked me to say. The place is busy enough as it is without more people discovering why it's so popular. There's music every night in the cellar bar (live on Tuesdays and Thursdays) and an excellent comedy club here on a Sunday, but it's so much more than that. The antithesis of the trendy wine bar, both tartlets and grunge-muffins have stumbled upon it, found it to their liking, and stayed for the ride. Vegetarian bar meals and dreadlocked bar staff, an atmosphere thick enough to inhale and Moles Club (run by the same mob) is just a hop, skip and a stagger away. Unbeatable.

Food 12-9 Mon-Sun

▪▪▪ The Roundhouse

Cheap Street – 425070

Location, location, location. This pub has it all. Unfortunately, it relies on location alone to pull in passing trade. Apart from the unusual architecture (it's round – hence the name) there's not a great deal going for the place. A melting pot of unsuspecting tourists and local sad cases keep the Roundhouse in business. My advice: go in, sup a quick pint, admire the architecture and move on.

Food 12-5 Mon-Sat

▪▪▪ Sam Weller's

Upper Borough Walls – 474911

Oh, it is so sad to see this. We know you have dreams, but you really should get a grip. You are not a cocktail bar Sam Weller's, and you never will be. You can put up your lovely 2-4-1 posters in the window; you can tell everyone about your lovely range of cocktails; you can hire some attractive bar staff, but we ain't buying it. A town centre pub with aspirations. Face facts Sam, you're only fooling yourself.

Food 12-9 Mon-Sat, 12-6 Sun

▪▪▪ The Saracen's Head

Broad Street – 426518

Legend has it that Charles Dickens wrote The Pickwick Papers during a stay here in the 1830's. The Saracen's Head claims to be the oldest boozer in Bath and has lots of signs on the wall and a display cabinet filled with old looking stuff to prove it. It's enormous inside, having been recently extended to cope with the volume of tourists who

come to savour the authentic olde worlde atmosphere complete with olde worlde fruit machines and olde worlde chart music.

Food 11-10 Mon-Thu, 11-8 Fri & Sat.

▪▪▪ Smith Brothers

11 Westgate Buildings – 330470

Always the first stop for any stag party, Smith Brothers is full of lads every night of the week. It's a spacious place with a couple of pool tables upstairs and, more often than not, an entertaining fight outside at closing time. If your idea of a great night out is listening to drunken wide boys pretending to be Robbie, then don't miss karaoke night on a Friday. Let Me Entertain You? No thanks mate.

▪▪▪ The Star

The Vineyards – 425072

Favourite of the boys in blue, you can guarantee a trouble-free night here unless you're planning to chin any of the regulars and then you'll be nicked, mate. The Star is just one of 30 National Heritage pubs. Untouched by the 21st and even the 20th century. Fruit machines and jukeboxes are conspicuous only by their absence. Do take time to check out the Small Bar; there's a long bench here known as Death Row and if you reach up to the shelf above you can still find tins of complimentary snuff.

MORGAN'S SPICED

A MELLOW MIX OF SPIRIT AND SOUL THAT FLAVOURS WHATEVER IT TOUCHES.

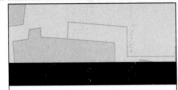

www.itchybath.co.uk

■ ■ ■ Babylon
Kingston Road - 400404

Run by the Karanga boys, you can guarantee that the music will be excellent. It's a busy place, with lots of nooks and crannies to snog in, and lots of beautiful people to snog with. The drinks are reasonably cheap too and there are usually special 2-4-1 promotions, and the bouncing atmosphere kicks off every night without fail. Like the blue Babylon, we need them to keep this city in order, but unlike boys in blue, they dance to salsa on a Tuesday and indie/punk on a Thursday.

■ ■ ■ Cadillacs
90b Walcot Street - 464241

Have you ever thought to yourself, what I really want is a night out in a mainstream club, listening to mainstream music surrounded by forty-year-old Barbie dolls? Yes? Well your night will start and end here. Friday nights at Caddies are locally known as 'Bag-A-Slag' night. The booze is as cheap as the company. Nuff said.

■ ■ ■ The Fez
7a Bladud Buildings - 444162

Expect sandstone walls, big mosque shaped red cut-outs and huge queues for the bar. All sounds a bit cheesy? Yeah, I suppose it is, but aside from that there's great music, lots of

Finger tips

RIZLA It's what you make of it.
www.rizla.com

Babylon
Kingston Road, Bath.
Tel: 01225 400404

Tuesdays: Salsa Night
Class from 8.30pm - Beginners & Improvers
9.30pm - Improvers & Intermediates
10.00pm Onwards - Salsa Music
Doors: 8.00pm - 1.00am
£4.50 / £3.50 NUS

Wednesdays: Cocobanana
The Biggest Student Night in Bath
Starts late September
Keep your eyes peeled for further info!

Thursdays: Discord
From Indie to Punk & back
Doors: 9.30pm - 2.00am
£4.00 / £3.00 B4 11.00pm / £2.00 NUS

Fridays: Superfly
70s Funk & Disco
Doors: 9.30pm - 3.00am
£5.00 / £3.00 B4 11.00pm

Saturdays: Relentless
Devilishly Delightful Dance Music
Doors: 9.30pm - 3.00am
£5.00 / £4.00 B4 11.00pm

spots to get away from the music if you just fancy a late night drink, a pool table and best of all, lots of chill out areas that consist of Moroccan-style seat-cum-bed thingies that are just too perfect for copping off with that beautiful blonde on. Over 21s only.

■ ■ ■ Moles
14 George Street - 404445

You have to visit Moles. That's an order. Forget the rest and head straight for Moles. You'll regret it if you don't. When you return home after your night/week/month in Bath, all your mates'll say, 'Did you check out Moles?' and you'll have to hang your head in shame as you admit that no actually you didn't. They'll seize on your weakness and follow this up with tales of what it was like when they went to Moles. They'll tell you of the time they saw Blur here, of the time that Gabrielle popped in for a quick sing-song. They will rave about the beer, and the time they got off with one of Bath's beautiful people. In short, they will mock you mercilessly for not being cool enough to have gone to Moles. You will be known as the one who didn't go to Moles. Eventually your confidence will be eroded, you'll find yourself having anxiety attacks, followed by clinical depression and before you know it you'll be too screwed up to leave the house. You'll become a sad statistic and die a lonely death surrounded by your twenty-six alphabetically named cats. Get the picture?

Hot tip

■ ■ ■ Pavilion
North Parade – 316198

The Karanga boys organise some cracking nights at the Pavilion on a monthly basis. The top names in music grace this small venue and educate the masses. The likes of Judge Jules and Brandon Block have all performed here. Nights take on several styles of music and a variety of theme names, kit yourself out in that old school uniform or fulfil your fantasies with 2-Kool for School, Boogie Wonderland and other Karanga special nights. Tickets to each event can be bought from Bar Karanga on Manvers St, Replay Records, or you can call 0870 4444 400 for credit card bookings.

■ ■ ■ Po Na Na
8 North Parade - 401115

One of the better examples in the Po Na Na chain, this place attracts a fair crowd most nights of the week, with queues stretching round the corner at weekends. If you're plan-

ning a night out here then have those last few drinks at neighbouring Lambrettas Bar; it'll allow you to keep one eye on the queue. The club is in the vaults so there's a real party in a cave vibe. The management inform us that it's due for some redecoration (and not before time - they've taken that shabby-chic thing as far as it can possibly go) so if you see a sign that says 'Wet Paint', just remember that it's not an instruction.

■ ■ ■ Savilles
Saville Row - 425550

More of a late-night drinking den than a club. It's small, so if you're thinking of going on Friday or Saturday then don't bother - it'll take you 'til 2am to reach the bar. But for a weeknight late drink it's pretty much unbeatable, with fairly decent music and a pool table upstairs. That, and the sexiest barman in Bath, makes it rightly popular with the locals. If you can find the place (it's well hidden), just knock on the door to gain admittance.

■ ■ ■ T's Club
Spring Gardens Road - 425360

Formerly the Tiergarden, T's has cast off that label and is building a firm reputation as an Indie paradise. Set in vaults and heaving on the weekends, this is a popular student haunt. Cheapish drinks, scary bouncers, bar staff who are completely off their faces and the obligatory drunk female student in the bogs sobbing about how all men are bastards. It's not the biggest club in the city, but that's a good thing, as even on slow nights it doesn't feel empty. We like it.

RIZLA✚ It's what you make of it.

club listings

For more up-to-date reviews, previews and listings check www.itchybath.co.uk

All listings details are subject to change at short notice, and therefore be used as a guide only.

Club	Night	Music	Price	Close
MONDAY				
Cadillacs	Student night	commercial chart	£1.50 – £2.50	8.30-2am
Fez Club	The Spanish Way	Spanish pop	£3	9-2am
Po Na Na	Love Lounge	breakbeat / big beat	£1 / -	9-2am
Moles	Monday Live	live bands/DJ's	£2 – £3	9-2am
Savilles	General night	hip hop, jungle, house	Free	7.30-2am
TUESDAY				
Babylon	Salsa night	salsa	£3.50 – £4.50	8.00pm-1am
Cadillacs	Hire only	-	-	-
Fez Club	Dogma - student night	r&r, hip hop,trance & house	£2.50/ -	9-2am
Po Na Na	Glamour Puss	60's-80's mix	-	9-2am
Moles	Big Cheese	60's-80's mix	£2 – £3	9-2am
Savilles	General night	hip hop, jungle, house	free	7.30-2am
WEDNESDAY				
Babylon	Cocobanana	student night	-	9.30-2am
Caillacs	Hire only	-	-	-
Fez Club	Loaded - student night	house/breakbeat	£2 / £1 for ladies	9-2am
Moles	Mr Phats	funk	£2 – £3	9-2am
Po Na Na	Drive By	drum & bass	-	9-2am
Savilles	General night	hip hop, jungle, house	Free	7.30pm-2am
THURSDAY				
Babylon	Discord	indie, punk and back	£2 – £3	9.30-3am
Cadillacs	Pound Night	commercial chart	£2.50 – £3	9-2am
Fez club	Back to the Floor	Soul, hip hop, house	£3/-	9-2am
Moles	Lost in the mix	indie/punk/alt	-	9-2am
Po Na Na	Saucy	hip hop - house	-	9-2am
T's club	Student night/Chart	commercial chart	£2 NUS, £3.50	9.30pm-2am
Savilles	General night	hip hop, jungle, house	Free	7.30pm-2am

Flick through the papers

Club	Night	Music	Price	Close
FRIDAY				
Babylon	Superfly	70's funk, and disco	£3 – £5	9.30-3am
Cadillacs	General night	chart/dance	£4.50	9-2am
Fez Club	Funky Monkey	house & funky night	£3 – £5	9-2am
Moles	Elixir	pure dance	£3 – £4	9-2am
Po Na Na	Fat Friday	funky house/disco	-	9-2am
T's club	Student night	eclectic mix	£3.30 – £4	9.30-2am
Savilles	General night	hip hop, jungle, house	£2/-	7.30-2am
SATURDAY				
Babylon	Relentless	house night	£4 – £5	9.30-3am
Cadillacs	Saturday night party	eclectic mix	£6	9-3am
Fez Club	Funk	funk, reggae, house & hip hop	£3 – £5	9-2am
Moles	Live Acts	bands/dance DJs	£4 – £5	9-2am
Po Na Na	Saturday night	funky house/ big anthems	-	9-2am
T's club	General night	eclectic mix	£3.50 – £4	9.30-2am
Savilles	General night	hip hop, jungle, house	£2/-	7.30-2am

Best places for:

House and Garage: Relentless @ Babylon on Saturday

Funk: Mr Phat's @ Moles on Wednesday

Jazz: The Old Farmhouse Pub; Green Park Braz; Jazz Night @ Moles on Sunday.

Indie: T's any night; Discord @ Babylon, Mix or Purr @ Moles on Thursday

70's and 80's: Po Na Na on Tuesday; The Huntsman on Thursdays.

Pop: Cadillacs ; Saucy @ Po Na Na on Thursday

World Music: Salsa @ Babylon on Tuesday

Reggae: The Hat and Feather on Wednesday

Drum 'n' Bass: Drive By @ Po Na Na on Wednesday

Hip-hop and R 'n' B: Burn @ The Fez on Tuesday

Punk: Discord @ Babylon on Thursday

Big Daddy: Hip hop, beats and culture

Juice: The UK Garage Bible

Knowledge: Drum'n' bass and breakbeat

Straight no Chaser: Jazz and all things funky

Playlouder.com: Like NME but a lot better

RIZLA + www.rizla.com

cafes

www.itchybath.co.uk

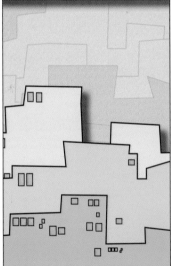

Adventure Café
5 Princes Buildings - 462038

Possibly the coolest place in the city to stop for a quick bite, The Adventure Café serves up natural, wholesome grub to natural, wholesome punters. Forget the tea or coffee – go for one of their fruit milkshakes or smoothies; they're homemade with fresh fruit and totally addictive. Better still, there's outside seating so you can spill out onto the pavement and watch the world go by continental-style.

Mon-Fri 8-5, Sat 9-5, Sun 10-5

Greenpeace sandwich (avocado, brie, sun-dried tomatoes and toasted peanuts)
£3.50-£4.25 depending on size.

Binks
17 Cheap Street - 445702

Don't get sucked in, this really is tourist trap territory. Binks stands in the shadow of the Abbey and with huge outside seating, attracts more than its fair share of gullible tourists. If you reckon it'd be a great place to stop and chat with the locals then think again. Nobody who lives in Bath goes here. The food is overpriced, the service is slow and the friendly atmosphere conspicuous only by its absence. If you're more than happy to munch rubbery food and sup luke-warm tea then you're going to love the place.

Sun-Fri 8-11, Sat 8-11.30

Fish and chips £5.95

enjoy the perfect cup...

coming soon to the city of Bath

COFFEE#1®
live coffee, love coffee

■ ■ ■ Café Cadbury
23 Union Street - 444030

Famous bad powit, Eric Nuff, found inspiration here. He penned his tribute to Hot Chocolate as he sat outside eating chocolate covered croissants and watching the world go by. For those of you who aren't familiar with his work, 'Ode to Hot Chocolate' goes like this:

It's frothy
It's not coffee
It can sing
You Sexy Thing

A genius at work, sucked in by the delicious chocolate aroma that filtered out onto the street forcing all but the hardened dieter to enter. If we were a naff guidebook then we'd be screaming Choctastic! at the top of our voices, but we're not, so we won't.

Mon-Sat 9-7, Sun 11-4

Hot Panini served with chocolate chilli chutney £3.95

!	🗋 🖉	From	Subject
!	✉	itchycity.co.uk	Meal offers by e-mail

■ ■ Coffee One
11 Old Bond Street

Under construction as we went to print. If the one in Cardiff is anything to go by, you can expect cracking coffee mixed into a chic environment with stylish décor, comfy slouching sofas and waiters and waitresses that can hold their own.

■ ■ Francis Hotel
Queen Square - 0870 400 8223

You may not be able to afford to stay here, but don't let that exclude you from the whole cucumber sandwich eating thing. The hotel is open to non-residents and serves up cake, coffee and finger sandwiches. Nicotine addicts aren't catered for, and no, you can't sneak a quick fag in the bogs if you're gasping. That's not the done thing at all, daaaarling.
Mon-Sun 9-6
Pot of tea and a toasted teacake £3.95

■ ■ Harington's
Queen Street -461728

On a summers Saturday this place is an absolute haven when the city is full to bursting and there are queues to sit in even the dingiest of dives. They do a cracking cooked breakfast, serve some bloody gorgeous muffins, and even go as far as providing freshly squeezed juice. Bang in the centre of the city, but tucked in a little side street – not many come across it, so you're pretty much guaranteed a seat – or at least you were 'til now. I may have to do a Salman Rushdie disappearing act when the locals discover I've blabbed about one of our best-kept secrets.
Mon-Sun 8-7
Somerset scones with clotted cream and jam £1.35

■ ■ Jazz Café
Kingsmead Square - 329002

Bright, cheerful, informal, unpretentious and looking out onto Kingsmead Square, The Jazz Café is another favourite of Bathonians. Hangover breakfasts are a speciality, so check out the Big Breakfast. It's served with huge doorsteps of toast and is just the thing to set you up for another night on the booze. By day, it's a casual little spot, but as evening falls they serve dead cheap themed dinners (Italian one week, Mexican the next) with special 'dine for a fiver' deals. Not bad value at all.
Mon-Sat 8-9, Sun 10.30-4
Bacon and Stilton toastie £3.50

■ ■ Lovejoys
7 Bartlett Street - 446322

It's quite a hike to get to this place, but it's worth every blister. If the walk hasn't cleared your head then the full English will. The cooked brekkies are probably the best in the city (they don't just cover your plate in baked beans and hope for the best), the service is efficient and the punters are mostly chatty sorts that have been hunting for or selling antiques at the Bartlett Street market. And with a decent cup of coffee too, this one's a winner.
Mon-Tue 9.30-4, Wed 8-4, Thu-Sat 9.30-4
Breakfast Bap £3.50

■ ■ ■ Tai Tai Teahouse
51 Walcot Street - 444122

Legend has it that Emperor Hui Tsun insisted that tea leaves should be picked by young virgins with gold scissors. In these days of mass production, I have a feeling that the tea served up by the Tai Tai Teahouse doesn't place such stringent requirements on its suppliers. That said, they do serve an impressive range of teas in a tranquil atmosphere. This is the only authentic Oriental teahouse

top 5 for...
Cheap Eats

1. Bottelinos
2. The Porter Bar
3. Central Wine Bar
4. Walrus and Carpenter
5. Adventure Café

in the country, and the owner, Niki, will even perform tea ceremonies if you book in advance – now that's something you won't see everyday. If you're feeling a bit hungry after all that then choose from the vast menu. You can have whatever you like - as long as it's noodles.

Tue-Sat 10-5.30, Sun 11-5.30

Noodles £3.99, Gunpowder tea £1.75

Instant
Direct
Cheap

Oi...Venue Managers
It takes 5 minutes to contact all your customers

We'll help you build a database of your customers, and give you a simple to use tool to send text messages – it takes no longer than five minutes to send a text to as many people as you wish.

It's cheap (£9 for 100 messages, less for more) and far simpler than designing, printing and distributing flyers. Plus, you know that it will be seen (and by who) and we won't pass on your customers details to anyone else.

For more information call us on **0113 246 0440**, or e-mail **venuemail@itchymedia.co.uk**

entertainment

www.itchybath.co.uk

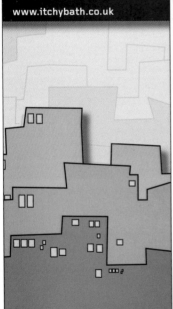

Cinemas

ABC Cinema
22 Westgate Street – 461730

Though by no means the smartest cinema you've ever been to, the ABC has character and thankfully they've done away with the uncomfortable seats that made visits here a nightmare in the past. All the big name films on general release show here.
Adults £4.90; NUS/kids - £3.50

Little Theatre Cinema
St Michaels Place – 466822

The owners of this little independent cinema are film lovers and are more than happy to chat knowledgeably about the programme before or after each screening. The choice of films is diverse, but consists mainly of foreign, specialist and independent features. An absolute gem with a huge local following.
Adults £4.50; NUS, £3.50; kids £3

Robins Cinema
St John's Place - 461506

With three tiny auditoriums (the largest has 200 seats, the smallest just 44), the multiplexes aren't exactly quaking in their boots. Robins shows mainstream films on general release, usually once they've finished play-

ing at the ABC. There are some great double-seats at the back, just perfect for snogging couples or chubbers.
Adults £4.20; NUS/kids, £3

■ ■ Theatre

■ ■ The Theatre Royal
Sawclose – 448815

Built in 1805, this Georgian theatre is the biggest and most popular in Bath. The interior has recently undergone renovation and the seating and legroom is much improved. Over the years, the likes of Anthony Hopkins, Glenda Jackson, Charlton Heston and even Olivier have played here. The theatre plays host to many London productions who preview here before moving onto the West End. The Shakespeare Festival in Spring is considered one of the best in the country, but The Royal is keen to allow modern productions to take centre stage and is no stranger to controversy; Shopping and F**king, God and Stephen Hawking (written by a local lad) and even Puppetry of the Penis (featuring two naked Australians playing with their genitals) have played here recently to full houses. The best seats in the house are those in the stalls and the Royal Circle, but if you're a bit skint then remember that a limited number of standby tickets are available from midday on the day of the performance for just £5 each. Standing tickets are available when the seats are sold out, and the advantage here is that you'll be first to the bar in the interval. There's two restaurants affiliated with the theatre: The Vaults and Prometheus. Both offer pre, or post, theatre dining.
£4-£28

■ ■ The Ustinov
Monmouth Street – 448844
Built from a donation by the great man himself, The Ustinov has an incredible programme of entertainment. The Puppet Festival is held here as well as workshops, children's theatre, devised performance, one-man shows, chamber music and smaller plays by local groups. The flexible performance space also makes this a popular spot for post-Edinburgh Festival tours from comedy players. The seating is comfortable, but do try and book in advance as the seats at the back can have you looking down on the performers heads.
£3.50-£15

■ ■ The Rondo
St Saviours Road – 444003
Under new management, The Rondo looks set to go from strength to strength. The building was originally a church, then a con-

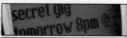

itchy sms @ www.itchybath.co.uk

cert hall before finally ending up as a theatre. You're as likely to find local groups experimenting with new works, as you are to find professional players performing Shakespeare. The stage is best suited to minimal settings making it a popular venue during the Bath Fringe Festival.

£4-£12

■ ■ Live Music

A live music section in Bath? If the current trend continues then expect itchy bath 2006 to contain a 'Places To Go To Avoid Live

Music' section. Almost everywhere you go in Bath you're accompanied by music. From fledgling rock bands to string quartets, if you're looking to sup a pint, do some shopping, eat a meal or stop for a cuppa, you're more than likely to find someone sticking their trumpet where they shouldn't.

So let's start in the morning. You're just out of bed and plan to hit the shops. Buskers abound on every corner, and you'll see and hear everything from a guy playing a saw to a barbershop quartet. Now you fancy stopping for a cuppa, Bath style. Music accompanies you in the **Pump Room**. Fancy a bit more bass than Beethoven? Head for the pubs. Try the **Hat and Feather** or the **Porter Butt** on the east side of the city or head for the **Porter Bar** on Tuesdays or Thursdays. If you can face the hill then **The Belvedere Wine Vaults** is a blast – there's a wonderful atmosphere and anyone with a guitar, a trumpet or a voice is welcome to stand up, join in and more importantly, enjoy themselves. In the same neck of the woods you'll find **The Farmhouse**, where jazz is belted out at mega-decibel levels three times a week. Another jazz venue is **The Green Park Brasserie**, home of Green Net cyber café, so you can surf the net, dine on Anglo-French cuisine and satisfy your eardrums with live jazz of a very high standard. **The Green Tree** in Green Street has been known to host blues afternoons on a Sunday, whilst **Windows Art Centre** in Lower Borough Walls is fast gaining an enviable reputation for live music – there's usually something going on there on a Friday or Saturday night. Give 'em a ring on (01225) 421700 and find out what they've got lined up. And if all else fails, head to **Moles** club – it's one of the premier live music venues in the West Country.

PLAN YOUR RESIGNATION TACTICALLY

■ ■ ■ Sport

■ ■ ■ Bath City Football Club
Twerton Park – 423087

Okay, so it ain't exactly Premier League stuff, but in a city dominated by rugby, 'The Romans' need all the support they can get. Tickets cost little more than a pint and with a stadium of 8800 that's rarely stretched, at least you'll be guaranteed a seat.

■ ■ ■ Bath Cricket Club
North Parade Road – 336255

Founded in 1859, Bath are the premier cricket team in the area. Playing in attractive grounds overlooking the river and with views of the Abbey, it's a decent spot to partake in a traditional British picnic and watch the lads in white playing with their balls.

■ ■ ■ Bath Racecourse
Lansdown – 424609

There's been horseracing up at Lansdown since 1874, and for a flat, uncommercial track, it's not bad at all. It's actually the highest track in the UK and is worth a visit for the incredible views alone.

Can't get enough? You'd better plan your visit to the city to coincide with **The International Music Festival** then. In fact, why not stay a month and sample the musical delights of the **Fringe** too – it's the biggest Fringe festival in England, second only to Edinburgh in the UK. Better still, why not move here permanently and you'll be able to catch the **Guitar Festival** and the **Jazz Festival** as well. House prices too high and local accents too dodgy? Fair point. Better make it just the weekend then. Well, if you can possibly make it to Opening Night when Victoria Park makes way for about a quarter of a million music lovers to enjoy food, drink, entertainment, fireworks and live music for free then you'll be made very welcome indeed – and if I spot you amongst the crowds then I'll buy you a pint.

For details on Bath's many festivals contact: The Bath Festivals Trust, 2 Church Street, Bath. BA1 1NL – tel. (01225) 463362 or check out **itchybath.co.uk**

REMEMBER, LEAVE ON A POSITIVE NOTE.

■ ■ ■ Bath Rugby Club
The Recreation Ground – 325200

Top class Premiership and European Cup rugby action. Fed up with not being able to sink a pint or two during the footy, get yourself down to the rugby, where you can drink continuously. An attractive ground and a clubhouse that fills with local rugby groupies (or slappers as they are more commonly known) after the match.

■ ■ ■ Bath Sports & Leisure Centre
North Parade Road – 462563

Swimming, squash, basketball...all the usual leisure centre activities in a tired, crumbling and frankly uninspiring environment.

■ ■ ■ Museums & Art Galleries

■ ■ ■ American Museum
Claverton Manor – 460503

The manor itself was built by Jeffrey Wyatville in 1820, and it was the site of William Churchill's first political speech in 1897. Claverton Manor opened as a museum in 1961 and shows the American way of life from colonial times as well as featuring regular temporary exhibits. The grounds are huge and perfect for picnics and each year they put on an Easter Egg Hunt and a Civil War Enactment. Both are great fun – the latter is most amusing after a few vodkas.

Open: Apr-Oct: Tue-Sun 2-5. Special opening times in Nov-Dec.
Admission: £5.50

■ ■ ■ Bath Abbey Heritage Vaults
Kingston Buildings – 422462

A visual and audio guide of 1000 years of history on the site including Anglo-Saxon artefacts, and the rather creepy skeleton of a woman who was buried with the monks.

Open: Mon-Sat 10-4
Admission: £2

■ ■ ■ Beckford's Tower
Lansdown Road – 422212

This Grade I listed 154-foot tower was built for William Beckford in 1827. Beckford was a scholar, a novelist, an eccentric and more importantly he was seriously loaded and could afford to create his own tower to use as a library for his collection of rare books, and as somewhere to entertain his mates. Climb to the top – there are fabulous views. He must have thrown one hell of a party back in the good old days.

Open: Sat-Sun 10.30-5 during the summer.
Admission: £2.50

"WHEN YOU'RE SACKED, YOU CAN WORK FOR ME"

∎∎∎ Costume Museum
Assembly Rooms – 477789

The Costume Museum offers a fascinating insight into fashion over the centuries. All exhibits are original pieces. Check out the silver tissue dress from 1660. If that's a bit before your time then rest assured, there are modern designs too; each year since 1963 a leading fashion expert has chosen a piece for inclusion in the collection.
Open: Mon-Sun 10-5
Admission: £4

∎∎∎ East Asian Museum
Bennett Street – 464640

Exhibits date from an incredible 5000BC right up to modern times. The museum covers art from the Eastern world and features many hands-on activities. There are some fabulous stone and jade carvings here.
Open: Apr-Oct Mon-Sat 10-6, Sun 10-5;
Nov-Mar Mon-Sat 10-5, Sun 12-5
Admission: £3.50

∎∎∎ Hotbath Gallery
Hot Bath Street – 328673

Opened in 1994, this gallery features regular exhibitions of sculpture, applied arts, crafts, design, paintings and almost everything in between.
Open: Mon-Fri 9-4.45, Sat 10-4
Admission: FREE

∎∎∎ Jane Austen Centre
Gay Street – 443000

Centre dedicated to Bath's famous authoress. Surprisingly, she allegedly despised the city, but unsurprisingly they gloss over this little fact. Set in a little Georgian house, there's even the opportunity to have your picture taken in period clothing, an unusual service that is not without its uses. Post the pic back to mum and quell her fears about your debauched lifestyle.
Open: Mon-Sat 10-5.30, Sun 10.30-5
Admission: £3.95

∎∎∎ Microworld
Monmouth Street – 333003

You know the deal – they advertise as the most amazing and incredible place to go in Bath. You don't believe the hype and you walk on by. Stop. This place really does live up to all expectations. An exhibition of sculptures so small that you need a microscope to view them. The artists train themselves to carve these tiny marvels between heartbeats. Absolutely and unequivocally amazing.
Open: Mon-Sun 10-6
Admission: £3.95

BEWARE OF THE VOICES. FOR CAREER ADVICE WORTH LISTENING TO, INCLUDING **HELP** WITH **INTERVIEWS**, VISIT monster.co.uk

■ ■ ■ Postal Museum
Broad Street – 460333

The first postage stamp, the Penny Black, was issued from this building on the 2nd of May, 1840. Follow the history of mail delivery from 2000BC to the present day. The place is usually full of avid stamp collectors who have failed to recognise that there's a fine line between a hobby and mental illness.

Open: Mon-Sat 11-5, Sun 2-5
Admission: £2.90

■ ■ ■ Royal Crescent Museum
1 Royal Crescent – 428126

An insight into 18th century life. The house has been restored to appear exactly as it would have in Georgian times, with hand painted wallpaper, period furniture, artefacts and an incredibly realistic kitchen complete with mousetraps.

Open: Feb-Oct Tue-Sun 10.30-5; Nov Tue-Sun 10.30-4
Admission: £4

■ ■ ■ Roman Baths
Pump Room, Stall Street – 477785

An audio tour will guide you through the history of the Roman Baths. The remains of the complex are amazingly well preserved and include exhibits such as the gilt-bronze head of the statue of Minerva and the stone relief of the Gorgons Head, as well as smaller artefacts such as coins and mosaics. Wheelchairs (and their users) are admitted to the terrace overlooking the great bath for free. Pop next door to the Pump Room restaurant where you can sample a glass of real Bath water. How does it taste? Like bathwater. Gross. Not even a shot of gin could save it.

Open: Nov-Feb 9.30-5.30; Mar-Jun 9-6; Jul-Aug 9-10; Sep-Oct 9-6
Admission: £7.50

■ ■ ■ Sally Lunn's Museum
North Parade Passage – 461634

Small museum beneath the tearooms. Check out the stalagmites and stalactites as well as Roman, Saxon and Medieval remains, then pop back upstairs for a bun and a caffeine fix.

Open: Mon-Sat 10-4
Admission: 30p

■ ■ ■ Victoria Art Gallery
Bridge Street – 477233

This gallery boasts work by Gainsborough, Farrington and Barker, as well as hosting regular temporary exhibitions featuring various mediums including applied arts, photography and local works.

Open: Tue-Fri 10-5.30, Sat 10-5, Sun 2-5
Admission: FREE

■■■ Things to See & Do

■■■ Bath Balloon Flights

London Road – 466888

There's no better way to see the city than launching from Victoria Park with a camera in one hand and a glass of bubbly in the other. Treat a loved one who is scared of heights to the trip of a lifetime. They may well hate you for it at the time, but the memory of them clinging desperately to the sides of the basket before spewing their guts up over the city will amuse you for years to come.

■■■ Bizarre Bath

Leaving from The Huntsman – 335124

The maddest of the walking tours. Expect to find yourself hopping across Great Pulteney Street, throwing rabbits in the weir, locking people in the stocks, and being generally entertained for over an hour by complete nutters. All good fun and a pleasant change from all the Roman and Georgian stuff that you've already overdosed on. Recommended.

8pm during the summer, £4.50

■■■ Comedy Cavern

The Porter Bar, George Street – 424104

Now that The Fez Comedy Club has left this fair city and relocated to somewhere far flung like Poland (where by all accounts, they are crying out for a good laugh), the Comedy Cavern is the only regular comedy night in the city, and that's no bad thing. The small venue is perfect for stand-up and the standard of the acts is high, featuring big names, Edinburgh Festival previews and the occasional bit of local talent.

Sun at 8pm, £5

■■■ Ghost Walks

Garricks Head – 463618

These ghost walks leave from the pub and take around two hours to complete. They're not a bad way to get your bearings and hear a little about the history of the city. Listen to the infamous tale of the Man in the Black Hat amongst others. Be afraid. Be very afraid. The undead are all around. Oh really? Why can they never be arsed to turn up for the walk then?

Mon-Sat at 8pm, £4

!	🗋	🖉	From	Subject
	✉		itchycity.co.uk	Gig news via e-mail

■ ■ Guide Friday

Bus Station - 444102

Bus tours leaving from the bus station. They take in all the usual sights and the guides are very knowledgeable. An advantage here is that you're able to hop on or off the bus to take a closer look at the sights, and then wait for the next bus to continue the tour.

Every half hour from dawn 'til dusk, £3-£8.50

■ ■ Laugh in Bath

Grand Parade

These bus tours leave from Grand Parade (near The Empire) at regular intervals. This tour will take you past all the popular sights whilst simultaneously entertaining you with humorous histories of Bath's famous residents, visitors and local legends. Bath without the boring bits. Highly recommended. Every 20 mins from dawn 'til dusk, £3-£10 – if they aren't busy then make 'em an offer.

■ ■ Mayor's Walking Tours

Guides Office, The Pump Room – 477786

Free walking tours of Bath leave from outside the Pump Room. The guides are local people who give their time for free, so you'll be led around the city by someone who is not only knowledgeable, but also passion-

ate about the city. More importantly, they will happily point you in the right direction of the better pubs and restaurants.

Usually at 10.30 and 2.30 during the summer, FREE

■ ■ Parade Gardens

Grab a deckchair and sit down by the river. The locals are rightly proud of Parade Gardens; in the summer, the floral displays are absolutely magnificent with glorious themed topiary creations. It's worth a visit on a Saturday to escape from the crowded shopping area, and on a Sunday you may be lucky enough to catch a brass band or similar playing at the bandstand.

■ ■ Pulteney Bridge

Cameras out, folks. Pulteney Bridge is an extraordinarily pretty little shop-lined bridge that overlooks the weir. The bridge was designed by Robert Adam and is one of only three shop-lined bridges in the world. Impressed? You should be.

■ ■ Royal Crescent

Built between 1767 and 1775, The Royal Crescent is the work of John Wood the Younger. Over the years this magnificent

top 5...
Tourist Attractions

1. Roman Baths
2. The Abbey
3. The Royal Crescent
4. Microworld
5. The Costume Museum

crescent has been home to many famous residents including the Duke of York and the Prince of Wales, sons of George III. Originally divided into thirty mansions, most have been converted into plush, overpriced apartments that are highly coveted by wealthy Americans who fancy owning somewhere with a prestigious address. It's also home to a hotel and a museum.

■ ■ Sydney Gardens

This is the oldest park in the city and is listed as a Grade II park, meaning that its historical importance has been noted at national levels. The twelve acres of parkland were laid out in 1795, and it remains a picturesque

setting for a picnic or stroll. There are some tennis courts up there and, although they aren't in the best nick, they are free to play on. A beautiful spot during the day, but short cuts across the park after dusk aren't recommended unless you are a looking for thrills in the gents.

■ ■ Victoria Park & Botanical Gardens

Overlooked by the Royal Crescent, and featuring botanical gardens, a play area, a duck pond, a bandstand, tennis courts, a putting green, a golf course, some fine trees, a skateboard park and delightful bedding displays, this is well worth wandering down to when the crowds in the city get a bit too much. Entertainment, festivals and open-air concerts are regularly held here much to the disgust of the nearby residents who complain tirelessly that it is all so horribly loud.

■ ■ Days Out

■ ■ Longleat

Okay. Let's be honest. What image does Longleat conjure up for you? Is it: a) A beautiful stately home set amidst impressive gar-

this TXT and
free B4 11.30

itchy sms @
www.itchybath.co.uk

dens; b) The first safari park in the UK featuring the famed Lions of Longleat or c) Home of the affectionately named, Loins of Longleat, Lord Bath? It's c) isn't it? Because let's face it, as Lords go, he's pretty high up in the cool stakes. Not only does he reside in the biggest bachelor pad in the country, he also has a harem of wifelets to keep him company and provide more than enough inspiration for his Karma Sutra mural (which is on display in the house, should you be interested). This guy knows how to have a good time, and he'll make damn sure you do too. Whether you visit for the fine stately home, the magnificent gardens, the mazes and rides or for the safari park, there'll be something that appeals. Fancy a laugh, then follow a BMW into the monkey enclosure and watch as the little cuties remove the aerial and bumpers. Unbeatable entertainment.

Country town into a haven for weirdos and new-age hippies. Actually, they have a point. It's an absolute haven for the crystal-loving public so where better to pick up some new rune stones blessed by a genuine white witch wearing an Adidas tracksuit. And yes, we too were shocked to discover that Adidas was the witch's brand of choice. 'Spose all those traditional cloaks were a bitch to fit in the washing machine.

■ ■ Glastonbury

There are some who reckon that all Glastonbury has to offer is a muddy music festival every year and that Glastonbury has transformed from a quaint little West

■ ■ Stonehenge

Was it created by aliens as a landing spot for their futuristic crafts? I doubt it. Was it created by Druids as a place of worship? Certainly not. Was it created by crazed Welshmen as some sort of enormously heavy timepiece? Who knows? These and many more ridiculous questions will all go unanswered on the guided tour of Stonehenge. For those of you who have never been and never plan to, here's the blaggers guide: When your mates ask what it was like, tell them that you arrived at sunset, watched the rooks coming home to roost and felt an eerie sense of power surging through you, and then you can do like the rest of us do, and moan about the fact that they built a road so close

to it and the sound of the traffic was disturbing your meditation. Sorted.

■ ■ ■ Bristol

Bath's big sister. Bristol is just 10 miles away. They have big bars, big clubs, big shops, big festivals… you get the picture. It's big compared to Bath – but let's face it, everything is big compared to Bath. Bathonians hate it; they're just jealous. As luck would have it, itchy produce a rather excellent little guide to Bristol to help you get around. So don't leave it to chance, grab a copy and check it out.

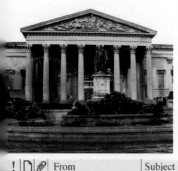

Jason, 28, owns Central Wine Bar

So where do you down a few when you're off duty? Central Wine Bar
Isn't that a little sad? Ever get out to eat? Yes, at Tilleys
Where do you shake your booty? In Bristol. Bath is crap for clubs.
And where are those snazzy clothes from? John Anthony
The best thing about this fine city? The architecture, the house prices (!)
And the worst? Rent and rates

■ ■ ■ Lacock

Okay. If we were from 'Puns 'R' Us' we'd be having a field day with this one. But sweetie daaaarling we are in Barrrrth and that sort of thing just wouldn't do at all. Lacock is a National Trust village just outside the city. There's invariably a film crew hanging around the village trying to film some period drama as residents are not allowed any external signs of 21st century life to adorn their properties. What do they do in the evening if they can't catch re-runs of Buffy on Sky? They go down to ye olde local pub of course and mingle with Americans who think it's all 'absolutely quaint'. For once they are probably right. Doesn't stop Americans being annoying, of course.

! ☐ ⧉	From	Subject
☐ ✉	itchycity.co.uk	Weekend offers to your inbox

shopping

www.itchybath.co.uk

Bath is an absolute joy to shop in. Coachloads of visiting tourists will tell you that. All the major chainstores are represented, yet a huge proportion of the shops are independents so you are guaranteed to find something a little bit different. But best of all, it's small, which means that you aren't trekking for miles to find what you're looking for. More time in the shops, less time walking between them.

■ ■ Walcot Street

Bath's bohemian boulevard; this area of the city is often missed by tourists who tend to stick to the main shopping area. Don't make the same mistake ; it's laden with some great independent stores stocking designer clothes, second-hand records, antiquarian books, futons, foodstuffs and practically everything in between. Better still there's a couple of class boozers to stop off at if your credit card needs a rest. Check out the flea market on a Saturday for bargains galore on everything from Tiffany glass to designer clothing. And you must visit if you're here during the Fringe Festival in June. Walcot Nation Day sees the whole street closed off to traffic and filled instead with music, great foods, street theatre, kids activities and enough beer to sink a ship.

■ ■ Southgate

In the shabbier part of town (though shabby for Bath is bleedin' posh to the rest of us) is Southgate. It's next to the train and bus station so it's probably the first impression that you'll get of the city, which is a bit of a shame. You'll find the cheaper chainstores and cut-price goodies here along with

McDonalds and KFC. It's all due for a bit of an overhaul but in Bath it can take years for the council to decide on anything, so no-one's holding their breath.

■■ The Podium

Okay, it's hardly a huge American style mall, but it's the best we've got. The Podium houses the library, Waitrose and a number of independent retailers stocking pretty much everything from fine arts to street fashions. Upstairs you'll find a number of decent restaurants including the California Kitchen who serve food all day. Oh, and there's a fabulous flower stall outside that has some very unusual specimens – definitely worth a look.

■■ Shires Yard

The entrance to Shires Yard can be found at the top of Milsom Street. It's a classy little number housing designer boutiques, jewellery stores and the wonderful Alessi Gallery. Gold cards at the ready girls: if you're living on a permanent overdraft then don't even bother looking in here. If you've got cash to flash then it'll be gone sooner than you can say 'Blimey, £218 for a corkscrew'. Still, it's a gorgeous little arcade and you can reach Broad Street from here via a pretty courtyard.

■■ Green Park Station

A restored Victorian railway station featuring a variety of specialist shops and stalls. You can purchase stationery, cards, pictures, frames, prints, bags, belts, hats, records, books and clothes along with one or two other things that I've probably forgotten. The shops are open all week but the stalls are closed on Mondays. Parking is easy, as the Sainsbury's car park is at the station. There's a farmer's market on the first and third Saturdays of each month and if you are exhausted from all that shopping you can stop off for anything from a cup of coffee and a muffin to a three-course meal at The Green Park Brasserie.

■■ Department Stores

■■ Jollys
Milsom Street – 462811

Bath's House of Fraser store. This place has been going strong for over 165 years now and is a favourite amongst the moneyed in the city. There's enough designer gear to keep any wannabe pop star satisfied, a well stocked china department, a café and a hairdressers as well as that bloody perfumery where you can run the gauntlet as ladies with scary orange faces and painted on eyebrows attempt to spray designer pongs in your face.

■ ■ ■ Rossiters

38-41 Broad Street – 462227

This is shopping at its best. Rossiters has grown considerably over the years. It started life as a kitchenware shop and has morphed into a huge department store. It's managed all this without losing any character and you'll find yourself browsing through a series of tiny interconnecting rooms and exploring the shop via winding staircases. The shop is still owned by the same family that started the business over 40 years ago and when it comes to personal service, they know their stuff. You're quite likely to be offered a cup of tea or a glass of wine while you shop – now that doesn't happen at Argos.

■ ■ ■ Silcox, Son and Wicks

Kingsmead Square – 463933

This department store is another of Bath's gems. Here you can buy anything for the home from tiny wooden mice for less than a pound to bedroom sets worth thousands of pounds from the network of private rooms. They specialise in exclusive designs from manufacturers here and abroad and stock some pretty funky stuff for the home.

■ ■ ■ Clothes – Women

The list may look depressingly short, but bear in mind that Bath's best stores are unisex so don't forget to check our unisex listings before you cancel the shopping trip. In addition to the independents, all the best known chainstores are represented in Bath.

■ ■ ■ Dressing Room

7 Quiet Street – 330563

Designer lingerie from Dior, La Perla, Marie-Jo, Aubade, Cotton Club and Hanro. They do a nice line in diamante-clad negligees if that's your particular bag.

■ ■ ■ Image

Shires Yard – 447359

Image specialise in designer clothing for the younger end of the market. That would be the younger and richer end of the market as you could buy a house in Bradford for less than the cost of a pair of trousers here. Clothes by Max Mara, MacLeod, Amay Alzuaga among others.

■ ■ ■ Long Tall Sally

Grand Parade – 466682

Fashion for leggy ladies.

■ ■ ■ Square

Shires Yard – 464997

Designer labels including Ghost, Joseph and McQueen. If you have to ask how much it costs then you can't afford it.

IT'S THE MD

■ ■ ■ Mrs. Simpson
Kingsmead Square – 461518

Credit card looking decidedly knackered? Check out this shop for a range of nearly new designer wear. Bargains galore.

■ ■ Oasis
2 Cheap Street – 442922

Funky, modern clobber for the more discerning girlie high street junkie.

■ ■ Whistles
Wood Street – 478984

Like Whistles in London, the shop stocks designer wear for the younger end of the market. Beautiful designs – big price tags

■ ■ Clothes – Men

Blokes in Bath don't have to go far to find decent togs. They can pick from the usual chains such as Burtons, Millets, River Island, Gap, French Connection, Next and Racing Green, which can all be found in the main shopping area of the city.

■ ■ Green Room
26 Broad Street – 315444

Skate and surf shop with clothing from Billabong, Rip Curl and Airwalk

■ ■ John Anthony
2 Quiet Street – 424066

Posh clobber for special occasions. Classy, well cut suits from Armani, Boss, Cerutti, Stone Island and Versace. Bargains to be had in the regular sales.

■ ■ Kitchi Gai
28 Broad Street – 465944

Casual designer wear without the hefty price tags. Check it out for Sonetti, Duck and Cover, Urban Stone and oh so many more.

■ ■ Clothes – Unisex

■ ■ Fat Face
6 Quiet Street – 446337

The Fat Face brand was started by a couple of surf bums. They stock funky casual gear as well as shoes at reasonable prices. Dangerously revealing changing rooms.

SHOW HIM YOU'RE NOT INTIMIDATED

■ ■ Gaff
Upper Borough Walls – 448585

Streetwear from the likes of Diesel, Firetrap, and Gas.

■ ■ Jack and Danny's
Walcot Street – 312345

Yeah baby! Austin Powers paradise. Designer garb from the 60's and 70's. Know exactly what you want but can't find it here? Don't give up. The shop is owned by a fashion designer and she'll knock up jeans or anything else to your exact specifications. Shaggadelic.

■ ■ Mayhem
6 Abbeygate Street – 315001

Denim heaven.

■ ■ Maze Clothing
19 Green Street – 448201

Check out their own label for quality, beautiful clothing or plump for something a little more expensive from Nicole Farhi. Proper, proper expensive.

■ ■ NSJ Levi Store
5 Abbey Green – 463803

Erm… they stock Levis. Now there's a shocker.

■ ■ Shoon
14 Old Bond Street – 480095

Okay – this is one place you have got to see. It's a whole shopping experience and worth blowing the budget for. Look out for brands such as Whitestuff, Tenson, Dockers, Belfe etc. It's mostly quality casual wear with a twist for both men and women but there are shoes, bags, sunglasses, jewellery and even artworks for sale too. Café upstairs.

■ ■ Walcot Woolies
Walcot Street – 463966

Wildly coloured home-knits for that 'I'm at one with the universe' look.

■ ■ WRC
Westgate Street – 447006

Streetwear from all the leading brands and a few unusual ones. Check out their own label brand for the best bargains.

■ ■ Zucci
7 Upper Borough Walls – 464392

Suits, suits and more suits. They stock the likes of Ted Baker, Paul Smith and Kenzo suits and shoes as well as ladies suits from Sandwich and Sand. This is also the only place in the UK other than Harrods that you can buy Canali suits. And guess what? They're cheaper in Bath. Just another good reason to shop here.

JUST KEEP SMILING AT HIM

■■ Footwear

All the major shoe companies are represented here so if you're looking for Dolcis, Clarks, Hush Puppies, Barratts and their ilk then you won't have far to look. If you are looking for something more unusual then read on...

■■ Duo
33 Milsom Street – 465533

Gorgeous Italian made shoes that you'll love so much you won't want to take them off. My boyfriend Mark doesn't get it though. "How can you be so in love with a pair of shoes?". Yeah, whatever.

■■ Jones The Bootmaker
19 Cheap Street – 465617

Kinky boots and other lovely shoes that Mark wouldn't understand about. Do I sound bitter?

■■ Mastershoe
92 Walcot Street – 460509

Masses of shoes including everything from cheap unbranded pumps to clumpers from Caterpillar, Doc Martins and Sketchers. They even have a welly section for people like

soleTrader

the ultimate range of designer and branded footwear

NIKE   BOSS HUGO BOSS
ted baker adidas DIESEL
FRENCH CONNECTION

9 Stall Street, Bath.
Tel: 01225 482040

Mark. Order your shoes at the till and they arrive in a cute little lift as if by magic.

■■ soletrader
9 Stall Street – 482040

The shop's as well designed as the shoes themselves. Whether you fancy loafing around town in the latest pair of must-have trainers, or causing a stir with your smarter choice of shoes or boots, you'll find something here to satisfy your every footwear whim. Take your pick from Timberland, Ted Baker, adidas, Buffalo, Diesel, French Connection, Camel, Hugo Boss, Acupuncture and Etnies, amongst many, many others.

BEWARE OF THE VOICES. FOR CAREER ADVICE WORTH LISTENING TO, INCLUDING HELP WITH INTERVIEWS, VISIT monster.co.uk

RIZLA ✠ WARE
QUALITY CLOTHING

■■■ Silvershoon
Upper Borough Walls

Silvershoon stocks mostly casual footwear with a twist. Brands include Ecco, Merrell, Think and Josef Seibel. These guys seem to have a talent for predicting what will be the next big thing and getting in before the rest catch up.

■■■ Music

■■■ Bath Compact Discs
11 Broad Street – 464766

Highly regarded as one of the leading independent classical music stores in the country, they do go the extra mile and if what you're looking for isn't in stock, they'll arrange to have it delivered directly to your door.

■■■ Duck, Son and Pinker
9-12 Bridge Street – 466586

Another independent store started years back by a musical hairdresser. Instruments, sheet music and an enormous noticeboard telling you exactly what is going on in the city. Worth a visit for that alone.

■■■ HMV
13-15 Stall Street – 466681

Chart CD's, tapes, DVD, video, posters. All the usual high street tunes, but with a compre-

hensive enough catalogue to satisfy all but the arsiest of musos.

■■■ MVC
Seven Dials – 311206

Voted best in Bath for helpful staff by Bath FM and the Bath Chronicle. There was no suggestion that family and friends rigged the poll. Huge selection of CD's, DVD's, videos, games etc.

■■■ Nashers
72 Walcot Street – 332298

If you can't find anything that takes your fancy amongst 80,000 records in this temple of second-hand vinyl then you're deaf. Some rare finds here and like any second-hand record shop worth its salt, there are decks to try before you buy, but only if you can prise off the local DJs hunting for new tunes.

■■■ Replay
27 Broad Street – 404060

Knowledgeable staff knocking out indie to dub reggae. Good jazz and second-hand section.

■■■ Subway
72 Walcot Street – 425376

House, hip-hop, drum 'n' bass. Some decent dance imports and staff that smile.

JUSTICE

BRITISH DESIGNER JEWELLERY

THE DOGS BRACELETS

BATH
16 Northumberland Place
OXFORD
12 New Inn Hall Street
WINCHESTER
80 Parchment Street

0845 601 0751
WWW.JUSTICE.CO.UK

■ ■ Books

■ ■ Booksale
Southgate Street – 464114
Cut price books covering all genres.

■ ■ Camden Books
146 Walcot Street – 461606

This place'll blow your mind. Floor to ceiling stacked with books. They're arranged over tables and stacked on the floor in random fashion. They've probably got exactly what you're looking for. It may take you two days to locate it, but it'll be there somewhere. Incredible. Mail order available.

■ ■ Good Buy Books
6 North Parade – 469625
General bookstore with knockdown prices. Best bargains to be had in the non-fiction department.

■ ■ Waterstone's
4-5 Milsom Street – 448515
This is the largest bookshop in Bath. Knowledgeable staff, a huge stock and a rather cool café on the top floor make it the most popular too. And that's not just because they stock this guide either. Ahem.

▪▪ WHSmith
6-7 Union Street – 460522

Decent selection of books on the upper floor, covering crime, horror, children's, cookery etc. WHSmith also have a second branch in The Mall, Southgate.

▪▪ Cool Shops

▪▪ Eureka
9-10 High Street – 462259

Check it out for ethnic wall hangings and wild and wonderful wooden statues spread over two floors.

▪▪ Faerie Shop
6 Lower Borough Walls – 427773

Fairy ornaments, fairy costumes, fairy dust and even adult size fairy wings that'll make the perfect gift for your mad auntie. Girlie heaven.

▪▪ Firebird
5 Queen Street – 339386

Everything from enamel jewellery to handmade shawls. Don't miss the cute little Russian bears; they're made of wood and have faces to die for. Well, they're maybe not worth killing yourself over when I think about it logically.

▪▪ Fudge Kitchen
10 Abbey Churchyard – 462277

Bloody gorgeous fudge from a store run by someone commonly referred to as 'a bit of a character'. Hang around looking undecided for a few free samples.

▪▪ Lotus Emporium
Guildhall Market – 448011

Top quality aromatherapy oils and other smelly stuff like soap and incense.

▪▪ Justice
16 Northumberland Place
(01225) 329300

The best jewellery in Bath. Inspired, modern ranges from Britain's finest young designers. Cool display stands, feasible price range and helpful staff who look like they know what they're talking about. A gem – no pun intended.

▪▪ Paddington and Friends
Abbey Street – 463598

The store is owned by Michael Bond – Padder's dad. Lots of memorabilia featuring the welly clad bear as well as other favourites such as Noddy, Pooh and Peter Rabbit.

▪▪ Stone The Crows
3 Broad Street – 460231

Transform your crappy bedsit into a funky studio – all it takes is a couple of wild mirrors, a clock in the shape of a dragon, a few throws and some huge soft cushions. Then throw a housewarming party and keep your guests entertained with the vast selection of 'oh so funny' practical jokes.

www.itchybath.co.uk

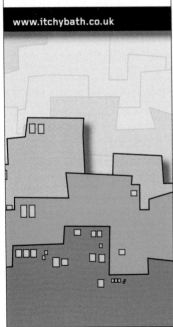

'Your mission, should you choose to accept it, is to find all those places in the city with extended opening hours...'
Come on mate, this is Bath we're talking about, not New York. It can't be done. Everyone here is tucked up in bed before midnight.
'I don't think Tom Cruise would have given up quite so easily...'
Not wishing to come off worse in comparison to that little short-arse, I took a deep breath, wiped the sweat from my brow and set off into the city on a mission impossible. (Fade in Mission Impossible theme tune: da da der der da da der der da da etc.)

■ ■ **Drink** – It'll cost you a couple of quid to get in if you arrive after 11, but you can grab a pint after hours at Savilles, The Huntsman and The Bath Tap. They all stay open until 2am. Alternatively you could try The Fez Club, which has a chill out area complete with pool table away from the music.

■ ■ **Just Come Out Of The Pub Grub** – There's nothing like a bag of greasy chips to soak up that alcohol. Check out Mr D. They serve until 1am during the week and a mind-blowing 3am on Fridays and Saturdays. Way to go Mr D. Kebabs after closing? Try the Kebab House in Kingmead Square open until 12.30am weekdays and 1am at weekends.

■ ■ **Restaurants** – You've pulled. She wants champagne and candlelight. You need a proper meal to keep your stamina up. Grab a table at The Wife of Bath, Woods, Tilleys, Pasta Galore, Hullabaloos or Pizza

Express… but you'd better hurry; last orders are 11pm. Didn't make it? Then dash along to Peking or Shangri La; they serve until 11.15, or make your way to Chopstick, Browns, Jamuna, Xian or Las Iguanas who keep serving until 11.30 or 12. After midnight you have a choice of Indian cuisine…or Indian cuisine: Rajpoot is open until 1.30am weekdays and 2am at the weekend.

■ ■ ■ **Late Night Shopping** – JCR minimart on the Upper Bristol Road is your first and last stop for all the after hours stuff you'll ever need: Pot Noodles, aspirin, condoms, can of cola, Rizlas and a packet of fags. Oh yes, you know how to romance a girl. Open 24 hours.

top 5 for...
Eating Late

1.	Rajpoot
2.	Jamuna
3.	Las Iguanas
4.	Chopstick
5.	Shangri La

■ ■ ■ **Cafes** – Teetotal? Really? Do you have any vices at all? The trouble with people with no vices is that you can be reasonably sure that they are going to have some pretty annoying virtues. Oh, you do have vices, but you just fancy a cuppa. Fair enough. 'Fraid your only option is Binks by the Abbey. It's open 'til 11.

■ ■ ■ **Attractions** – During July and August, the Roman Baths are open until 10, and the Baths by candlelight are particularly attractive. Highly recommended.

■ ■ ■ **Hair** – Hot date coinciding with a bad hair day? Phone up Factory in Julian Road. They're open 'til 6.30 but will squeeze

you in later if you sound pitiful enough. Toni & Guy'll snip 'til 7 during the week and you can rid yourself of those split ends at Supercuts until 7 on a Thursday. Blokes can get everything from a short back and sides to a professional barber's shave at Hacketts on a Wednesday and Thursday until a rather impressive 8pm.

■ ■ ■ **Beauty** – Hot-foot it down to The Orangery for late night beauty treatment; on Tuesdays and Thursdays they close at 7pm. Bath Beauty Clinic goes one better, opening until 7pm on Tuesday, Thursday and Friday.

Tom Cruise, eat your heart out. (Fade out Mission Impossible theme tune: da da der der da da der der da da etc…)
'You have done well, my son…'
(Fade in Karate Kid theme tune: der der dee dee der etc.)
It's a tough job, but somebody's got to do it. Time for my medication.

takeaway

www.itchybath.co.uk

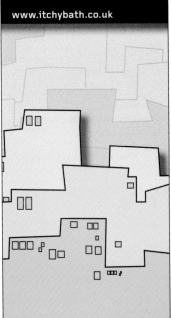

■■ Pizzas

■■ Bottelinos
Bladud Buildings – 464861
Best takeaway pizzas in the city.

■■ Pizza Kitchen
Wellsway – 429776
Takeaway burgers, pizzas, chips, drinks. Delivery service.

■■ Pizzarella
Chelsea Road – 339877
Pizzas, lasagne, chips, sausages, fish… you name it, they'll deep fry it and deliver it to your door.

■■ Burgers & Kebabs

■■ Kebab House
Kingsmead Square
They don't serve kebabs. Sorry, that's a lie. Late opening 'til 12.30am weekdays and 1am weekends.

■■ Marmaris
4 Grand Parade - 461946
Best kebabs in town for eat in or takeaway.

■■ Mr D
Monmouth Street – 426111
Upper Bristol Road – 425204
Not quite McDonalds. But that's a plus. Late opening.

■■ Schwartz Bros
Sawclose - 461726
102 Walcot Street – 463613
4 Sawclose – 461726
You can't go wrong with a Schwartz burger.

Fish & Chips

Ancient Mariner
Moorland Road – 420377
Chips. Good chips.

Seafood
Kingsmead Street – 465190
Fish, chips and beer to eat in or takeaway.

Twerton Chippy
Twerton High Street – 425920
Fish, chips and second-hand books for sale.

Indian

Curry Express
Augusta Place – 329111
Possibly the most unfortunately named curry house we've ever come across.

Desh
Chelsea Road - 314413
Popular spot for eat in or takeaway.

Moghul
Walcot Street – 464956
Can't find it? Just follow the curry slicks from the pub. Strange but effective advertising technique.

Chinese

Golden Dragon
Monmouth Place – 461172
Chinese, Cantonese and English dishes. Home delivery on Fri-Sun.

Cheong Sing
Moorland Road – 337117
Best beef chop suey in town.

Sarnies

Devon Savouries
Lower Borough Walls – 442099
Hot sausage roll and a can for less than a quid. That'll do nicely, thanks.

Fodders
Cheap Street – 462165
Bagels and buns. Open lunchtimes only.

Hardy's
Westgate Buildings – 316796
Bargain butties including peanut butter and jelly baguettes for our American cousins. And a great value breakfast baguette that deserves the title: Hangover Cure in a Bap.

Montgomery's
Queen Street – 338803
Sarnies made fresh to order.

Phipps Bakeries
3 Argyle Street
4 George St.
5 Orange Grove
68 Lower Bristol Road
The best bakeries in Christendom (except for that one in Paris near the Moulin Rouge).

accommodation

www.itchybath.co.uk

In Bath you're spoilt for choice – if you arrive in the winter. Summer, however, brings the crowds and it's wise to book in advance to avoid spending a cosy night with the crusties at the bus station. Visiting out of season is easier on the wallet due to the fact that every hotel and B&B in the city is desperately vying for your business. Prices are per person per night including breakfast.

■■■ Expensive

■■■ Royal Crescent Hotel
16 Royal Crescent – 823333
Five-star luxury in the centre of the crescent.
From £100

■■■ Lucknam Park
Colerne – 742777
The place where celebs come for r&r. You can even park your chopper (that's helicopter, not circa 1970s bike) on the front lawn.
From £110

■■■ Bath Spa Hotel
Sydney Road – 444424
If you can't afford it, content yourself with the fact that it used to be a scabby old hospital.
From £105

■■■ Queensbury Hotel
Russell Street – 447928
Georgian hotel with a cracking restaurant.
From £78

■■■ The Francis
Queen Square – 0870 400 8223
The Beatles stayed here once. Whatever happened to them?
From £70

■ ■ ■ Moderate

■ ■ ■ Haringtons
Queen Street – 461728
Right in the heart of the city.
From £44

■ ■ ■ Laura Place Hotel
**Laura Place, Great Pulteney Street
463815**
Excellent value.
From £35

■ ■ ■ Abbey Hotel
North Parade – 461603
Imposing, yet welcoming
From £60

■ ■ ■ Carfax Hotel
Great Pulteney Street
Georgian grandeur.
From £37

■ ■ ■ Brocks
Brock Street – 338374
Slap bang between the Royal Crescent and
the Circus
From £32

■ ■ ■ Budget

■ ■ ■ Bath Backpackers Hostel
Pierrepoint Street – 446787
Aussie run hostel with private rooms, kitchen
facilities, Sky TV, internet access, pool room,
late night bar, laundry room, hot showers and
best of all, no curfew. You'll need to flash a
passport to stay here and it's notoriously busy
so booking in advance is recommended.
From £12

■ ■ ■ YMCA
Broad Street Place – 460471
Location-wise, this is unbeatable. It's right in
the centre of the city, but tucked away down
a quiet street so you're unlikely to be woken
at 4am by marauding yokels. There's no curfew a decent gym, laundry facilities, steam
baths and a nursery. No booze though (shit).
From £11

■ ■ ■ Walton's Guest House
Crescent Gardens – 426528
Brilliant value just a stumble away from the
centre.
From £20

■ ■ ■ Romany
Charlotte Street – 424193
Clean, comfortable, central. What else do you
need?
From £18

■ ■ ■ Albany Guesthouse
Crescent Gardens – 313339
Centrally located accommodation at bar-
gain prices
From £17

useful info

www.itchybath.co.uk

If you're smart, you'll have decided that the bus fares are way too steep and the service far too unreliable and booked your cab in advance. You won't have reckoned for some scally nicking into your cab while you're air-kissing your mates goodbye outside the pub though, so join the crowds as they go in search of that elusive sight: the taxi rank without queues. Your best bet is heading towards the bottom of town to the rank next to the Abbey or the train station. Girls travelling alone should mention this fact when they call for a cab as they receive priority service, which extends to all pub and club owners being obliged to let them use the telephone to call a cab free of charge at the end of the night. Once you've bagged a cab, do go out of your way to strike up a conversation with the cabbie using the phrases: 'Busy tonight?' and 'So when are you knocking off?' They positively love that.

■ ■ Travel

■ ■ Taxis

AA Taxis	444441
Abbey Cars	444446
Coronation Cars	331298

Orange Grove Taxis 447777
Rainbow Taxis 460606
Station Taxis 425678

■ ■ Buses

Notoriously unreliable and probably the only thing in Bath that is more expensive than London. These services run from the central bus station at the bottom of town in Manvers Street.

Bath Bus Company 330444
First Badgerline 464446
National Express 0990 80 80 80

■ ■ Trains

All services run from Bath Spa station. The station itself has a car park, but it fills up quickly so do allow extra time to find alternative parking if you've got a train to catch. You can pay for your parking by swiping your credit card apparently, but the bloody machines never seem to work when we visit.

First Great Western 08457 000 125
Wales and West 08457 48 49 50
National Rail Enquiries 0345 48 49 50

top 5 for...

Hangover Breakfasts

1. Lovejoys
2. Jazz Café
3. RSVP
4. Hardy's
5. Haringtons

■ ■ Car Hire – Self-Drive
Avis 446680
Ford Rent-a-Car 402234
National Car Rental 481898

■ ■ Planes
Bristol International Airport
....0870 1212747
Cheap flights to domestic and European destinations offered by a number of operators including the budget airline, Go.

■ ■ Limousines
American Stretch Limos 709635
Chauffeur Link 446936

■ ■ Hospitals and Clinics

■ ■ Royal United Hospital
Combe Park – 428331
Biggest hospital in the former Avon region. There's a chronic pain clinic offering out of hours medical expertise as well as a busy A&E department, which is always good for a laugh on a Saturday night.

! ☐ 🖉	From	Subject
! ✉	itchycity.co.uk	Weekend offers to your inbox

There's better things to spend money on.
Don't waste it on travel.

If you're under 26 or a student save £££'s on travel with a Young Persons' Discount Coachcard. Cards cost £9 and save you up to 30% off already low fares all year. Register online to receive special offers throughout the year.

For journey planning, tickets and coachcards

visit **GoByCoach**.com or call 08705 80 80 80

NATIONAL EXPRESS ≫

Check online for details.
Coach services depart from Bus Station, Manvers Street, Bath.

▪▪■ Bath Clinic
Claverton Down Road - 835555

Small hospital more suited to face lifts than emergency treatment. Great for comedy value though, as they sell gift vouchers for operations. So now you can treat your bloke to a vasectomy for his birthday.

▪▪■ NHS Walk-in Clinic
Henry Street – 0845 46 47

Nurse-led health care with no appointments necessary.
Mon-Sun 7am-10pm

▪▪■ Other Useful Numbers

▪▪■ Tourist Information Office
Abbey Churchyard - 477101

What?!? We're not good enough for you now? Oh, you just want to pick up a few brochures… well that's okay then.

▪▪■ Bath Police Station
Manvers Street – 444343

▪▪■ Bath and NES Council
The Guildhall - 477000

Commonly known as BANES – we've yet to come across a more appropriate acronym for a council.

▪▪■ Media in Bath

Bath Chronicle: Award-winning local rag covering all the big stories from The Bath Pothole Crisis to tales of unlucky residents being crushed by falling lampposts. Okay –

Arron, 32, Bouncer at RSVP

When your name's down where do you drink? RSVP
And where do you fuel those biceps? Bottelinos
And where do you impress the ladies with some bouncer bopping? Po Na Na
And shopping? Everywhere
Everywhere that sells size 13s then. Best thing about Bath? Knowing everyone
And the worst? Nothing. Bath's great.

so they're slightly hampered by lack of news but they cope admirably, turning out some fairly comprehensive listings pages on a Wednesday.

Venue: Listings mag for Bath and Bristol. TimeOut for the West Country folk.

BathFM: Radio station with strong community links.

Galaxy: Dance radio spanning the South West and South Wales. Pretty standard commercial dance.

www.itchybath.co.uk: Up to date club listings, events, gigs, reviews, and text messages about forthcoming events. Available in 15 other UK cities. itchy guides in print are also available in 16 delicious flavours call 0113 246 0440 for more...

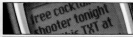

itchy sms @
www.itchybath.co.uk

index

!	🗋	📎	From		Subject
✉	✉		itchycity.co.uk		Weekend offers to your inbox

artificial intelligence • •

Available from Tesco, Waitrose and other leading wine and spirit retailers. Also available from Bar 38, Casa, Henry's, J D Wetherspoon, The Rat and Parrot, Via Fosse, RSVP and other independent bars and restaurants.

For more information call 020 8943 9526

www.seborabsinth.com

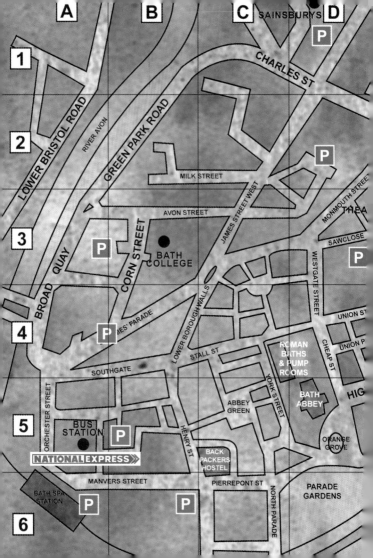